COUNTRY RISK

Assessment and Monitoring

COUNTRY RISK

Assessment and Monitoring

Second edition

Thomas E. Krayenbuehl

Woodhead-Faulkner
Cambridge

Published by
Woodhead-Faulkner Ltd
Simon & Schuster International Group
Fitzwilliam House
32 Trumpington Street
Cambridge CB2 1QY

First published 1985
Second edition 1988

British Library Cataloguing in Publication Data
Krayenbuehl, Thomas E.
　　Country risk: assessment and monitoring
　　2nd ed.
　　1. Debts, External　　2. Debts, Public　　3. Risk
　　I. Title
　　336.3′6　　HJ8015

ISBN 0-85941-409-4

Designed by Geoff Green
Phototypeset by Wyvern Typesetting Limited, Bristol
Printed in Great Britain by
St Edmundsbury Press, Bury St Edmunds, Suffolk

Contents

Part Four: Outlook

Preface

The international debt situation has, over the past few years, been one of the major items of discussion in the international financial community as well as in government circles. Many questions have been asked as to how the now familiar developments could have come about. While fortunately no great crash occurred, the international safety network established by the major central banks, the International Monetary Fund and the Bank for International Settlements had to be activated on more than one occasion. Working together with the governments of the debtor nations and with the co-operation of the internationally operating banks and some other governments, these institutions put into operation a very effective crisis management which weathered the different storms in a highly successful way. It would, however, be dangerously naïve to think that such situations will always be managed in a fairly smooth way. Rather, one should be asking the question: What more can be done in the future in order to avoid similar problems – that is, to find ways of managing the international debt situation with a minimum of crises? This question must be asked by all the participants in international lending and by international investors.

Borrowers realised that, under certain circumstances that are still difficult to quantify, their creditworthiness had suddenly gone. What are these circumstances? The importance of liquidity became apparent to sovereign borrowers which had before relied mainly on their high-solvency status. Furthermore, the effects of contagion have been underestimated. We still have no other explanation for the fact that all Latin American countries had to reschedule their debt within a period of roughly 12 months, even though there exist many differences between them in debt exposure per capita, export structures and national resources. One year before, the Eastern bloc faced a similar situation and was barely able to isolate the Polish and Romanian problems from the rest of its members. Sovereign borrowers will have to analyse their situations much more carefully in order better to detect what constitutes their creditworthiness in international financial markets – if they want or have to use them extensively.

Lenders and investors have also been made fully aware by the experience of the early 1980s that cross-border transactions incorporate an additional commercial risk for those usually associated with any lending or investment – the so-called country risk. By carefully evaluating and monitoring country risk, excessive lending or imprudent investments can be avoided.

The aim of this book is to give guidance to the international lending officer or investor on how better to assess and monitor country risk; it may also help students in banking to become acquainted with the subject. As the reader progresses, he will realise how complex the notion of country risk is. There is an almost endless number of factors that constitute and influence a specific country risk. From them must be selected those that are the prime movers for a quality change in a country risk, which means that countries with similar structures can be judged by considering similar factors.

The large number of factors and their mutual interdependence have so far not allowed the construction of convincing computer models to assess the behaviour of the quality of a country risk that produce better results than simpler assessment methods. This might change when essential country information is gathered at a faster pace with better-quality standards than today, so that many interrelations of the different data can be simulated for possible short- and medium-term developments. Still, those data will need interpretation, which requires not only a talent for logical deduction but also intuition and flair. The last two cannot be learned through reading but only either by living on the spot or by frequent visits to the country in question. Such visits must provide experiences that go far beyond those of a sales manager who calls on a client in a foreign country. However, slightly biased information or experiences might still be difficult to avoid.

The assessment of country risk is a demanding and fascinating task that in the future will have to make a much greater contribution in the evaluation process of cross-border lending and investment. Only then will the necessary realism based on a good relationship between risk and reward prevail and help break the current stalemate in many cross-border lending situations. If this book can further such a development, then one of its major objectives will have been achieved.

Assessment of country risk will make it possible to determine the quality of a country's creditworthiness but will not indicate the magnitude of advisable financial cross-border transactions for an institution. This will have to be done through monitoring, which must be based on the institution's decisions about its assessment of the country risk, its marketing goal for that country and its own risk-taking capability and willingness. Once those decisions are made, the monitoring itself will be to a large extent an administrative task. Some indications are also given in this book about how such monitoring might be organised. It will, however, depend very much upon the size of cross-border exposure, and upon the structure and complexity of the institution concerned.

Good assessment and correct monitoring of country risk are the twins that make cross-border lending and investment a successful exercise for every institution.

April 1985   Thomas E. Krayenbuehl

Preface to the second edition

Since I have written the Preface of the first edition of this book, two more years have passed. The international debt problem has lost some of its urgency for the international banking community as the major internationally operating banks have substantially increased their capital basis to weather better their exposure. Furthermore, under the leadership of Citibank, the money centre banks of the United States of America, and somewhat later also the British clearing banks, have begun making substantial provisions against country risk exposure following the example set by the banks from continental Europe. Also, the Japanese banks have started to take a more cautious view by selling part of their country risk exposure to a Cayman Island company owned by them in order to increase their provisions against country risk. The lenders are, therefore, in a stronger and more relaxed position than they were a couple of years ago.

The development on the borrowers' side has been much more heterogeneous. Most countries which had to reschedule in 1982 and 1983 had to make new rescheduling agreements in order to further stretch the repayment of their debt or to incorporate more of their total debt in the restructuring agreement through a so-called MYRA (multi-year-restructuring agreement) in order to obtain a better debt structure. Grace and repayment periods were prolonged while spreads were gradually reduced.

Over the past two years, the general economic environment was characterised by a good growth in the OECD countries. During the same period, most commodity prices declined. Interest rates did also fall. It is significant to note that, despite a generally better debt profile and a fairly positive worldwide economic environment, no country which had to reschedule its debt reached creditworthiness again in the last couple of years and, therefore, did obtain funds in the market. The different adjustment programmes adopted by the major debtor nations helped to avert insolvencies but failed to lead the different countries back to creditworthiness.

The only important initiative undertaken by the major lending nations to solve the international debt problem was the 'Baker Plan' presented by the US Secretary of the Treasury, James Baker, at the IMF Meeting in 1985 in Seoul. This initiative remained, however, only a work of words and never became a work of action.

It is, therefore, not surprising that a feeling of frustration has taken place among many major borrowing countries, because they cannot see an opportunity of breaking out of the vicious circle in which they find themselves. This has led to a hardening of the borrowers' standpoint by making unilateral decisions, such as limiting the amount of money available to service the debt or declaring a moratorium on debt payments. Furthermore, the need to make debt relief available has been voiced, not only by politicians in debtor countries but also in countries of lender nations. Of the different new initiatives launched to alleviate the debt problem, only the debt equity conversion programmes seem to be able to make some impact. The exit bonds, launched by Argentina in 1987, which would enable banks with minor exposures to opt out of the rescheduling process and possible new money requests have not been received in a very positive way, as the future marketability of these bonds is in no way assured. The same applies for the so-called Philippine Investment Notes (PINs) launched by Mr J Ongpin, Philippine Finance Secretary, in March 1987. These PINs are an interesting financial construction, but will only make an impact if their marketability is tested.

Despite this fairly negative development of the international debt problem with respect to the very highly indebted nations, international trade is continuing and has to be financed. This is also true for all the countries that had to reschedule their debt which, therefore, offer opportunities even if the country risk does not look very attractive. A correct country risk assessment is the only valid way which enables banks to judge the risk involved in such financing. The more intricate the situation presented, the more demanding the country risk assessment will become. Despite all the reschedulings, country risk assessment and monitoring has not lost any of its significance, but should be present whenever a cross-border exposure is contemplated.

For this second edition, I have rewritten part of the assessment procedure for political risk. Furthermore, I have updated all parts where I felt it necessary. In addition, I have added a chapter on debt/equity conversion programmes as it seems to me that such programmes have a potential to reduce the international debt exposure of several countries. I hope that these changes will prove helpful for the reader.

January 1988   Thomas E. Krayenbuehl

Acknowledgements

I would like to thank several people for the very valuable advice they have given on the writing of this book. Mr Guido Hanselmann, Member of the Executive Board of Union Bank of Switzerland, took a deep interest in my work and suggested changes and additions to the manuscript based on his long experience in international banking. My colleague Dr Bruno Gehrig reviewed the manuscript as a critical reader: his experience as a lecturer at the University of Berne influenced the final elaboration of the text in a very positive way. My colleagues Dr Klaus Huber and Dr Christopher Zenger gave me their informed opinion on the sections on cofinancing and logit analysis. Mrs Sheila Mary McKinley helped me to update the section on political risk for the second edition. A special debt of thanks must go to Mrs Sylvia Locher, who typed with great care the many drafts that led to the final manuscript. Mr Henry Isaac and Mr Thomas Logan offered me their advice on linguistic problems. Finally, I would like to thank very much Mr N. R. Wenborn, Commissioning Editor at Woodhead-Faulkner Ltd, for suggesting this book and following its progress. He and his colleagues gave me many suggestions beneficial to the finished work.

Part One
Overview

1

Introduction

Definitions

It would be useful at the outset to define some of the terms used throughout the book.

Country risk

Country risk is the possibility that a sovereign state or sovereign borrowers of a particular country may be unable or unwilling, and other borrowers unable, to fulfil their obligations towards a foreign lender and/or investor for reasons beyond the usual risks which arise in relation to all lending and investments. Country risk is composed of political and transfer risk.

Political risk

Political risk is the risk incurred by lenders and/or investors that the repatriation of their loan and/or investment in a particular country, i.e. capital, dividends, interest, fees or royalties, is restricted by that country for political reasons only.

Transfer risk

Transfer risk is the risk that a particular country may impose restrictions on remittances of capital, dividends, interest, fees or royalties to foreign lenders and/or investors as part of its economic policy.

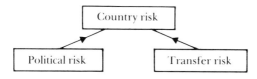

Sovereign risk

Sovereign risk arises from the special risk associated with a sovereign loan, which is a loan to, or guaranteed by, a government (or some government-guaranteed bodies). The special significance of such lending lies in the risk that it might prove impossible to secure redress through legal action – i.e. the borrower might claim immunity from process or might not abide by a judgement.

Country exposure

Country exposure is the amount of an institution's total investment and/or claims on borrowers in a specific country, directly as well as indirectly.

Country limit

Country limit is the numerical amount up to which an institution such as a bank or company is willing to take an exposure in a particular country.

Country rating

Country rating is the result of the individual appraisal of a particular country in view of its standing to honour its foreign debts in relation to other countries or groups of countries.

Direct country risk

Direct country risk in cross-border lending and/or investment is the country risk of the country where the borrower takes up his liabilities and/or the investment is made.

Indirect country risk

Indirect country risk in cross-border lending and/or investment is the country risk of the guarantor or of the main security if guarantor or security is in a different country than the one where the borrower has taken up his primary liabilities or where the investment has been made. The lender qualifies this risk as his ultimate country risk.

Rescheduling

Rescheduling is a process by which the lender and the borrower agree to arrange new conditions for an existing loan agreement.

Moratorium

A moratorium is the unilateral declaration of the borrower that he is unable and/or unwilling to honour all or part of his obligations and thereby stops the servicing of his debts. It is a breach of contract.

Historical background

In 1982 and 1983, country risk assessment and monitoring entered a stage of reality not anticipated some years ago. While until 1981 reschedulings had occurred from time to time and on a fairly limited basis (except for Turkey), the situation has radically changed since; today nearly all countries of Latin America, as well as many countries in Africa, have been passing through the rescheduling process. Most of these countries have, since 1984, made several debt restructuring agreements as they were not in a position to resume normal debt servicing. In some cases, so-called MYRAs (multi-year rescheduling agreements) were concluded in order to stretch the repayment of the debt that was not yet even due at the time the agreements were concluded. The restructuring agreement made it possible for the countries in question to resume their debt servicing according to the agreement. In 1985, a new element came into play when President Garcia of Peru suddenly declared that Peru will, in the future, only use ten per cent of its export earnings for servicing its debt. This moratorium was considered an exceptional action. However, since Brazil declared, in February 1987, a moratorium on 68 billion US dollars of its medium- and long-term debt, other countries followed. At the time of writing, several countries, such as Peru, Brazil and Ecuador have taken such a unilateral step *vis-à-vis* their creditors.

Debt restructuring agreements were signed with commercial banks between 1982 and 1987 as indicated in Table 1.1.

Rescheduling is just one step – but an important one – in the deterioration of a country risk. For the country involved it is, however, the first step towards an improvement in its financial situation. If we look at the size of the figures currently under rescheduling, we can even say that a substantial part of the assets of cross-border lending has lost some of its quality. In their original quality these assets were considered to be repayable at due date without any question. This is no longer the case, even for the rescheduled amounts, as some countries have declared a moratorium for their debts. How did all this come about?

Today's situation is the outcome of an exceptionally intensive growth in international lending since the beginning of the 1970s. International lending, however, is not an invention of the last 15 years; it has been going on for centuries in one way or another. The Medici banking family was highly successful in international lending in the fourteenth and fifteenth centuries. In the early sixteenth century, the Fugger family from Augsburg was heavily involved in financing the popes and the Austrian emperor. It lost substantial sums due to the difficulties the emperor had with his Spanish finances. The Rothschild family is another example of success in international banking. With its different banks in the major capitals of

Table 1.1. Debt restructuring agreement with commercial banks, 1982–87

Year	Debtor countries	Amounts restructured (in US$ million)	New money
1982	Guyana	15	
	Liberia	27	
	Nicaragua	100	
	Poland	4,500	200
	Romania	1,598	
1983	Bolivia	514	
	Brazil	20,475	4,400
	Chile	4,826	1,300
	Costa Rica	650	225
	Cuba	620	
	Dominican Republic	498	
	Ecuador	2,535	431
	Mexico	25,000	5,000
	Malawi	76	
	Nigeria	1,935	
	Peru	2,380	450
	Poland	1,045	150
	Romania	572	
	Sudan	790	
	Togo	84	
	Uruguay	662	240
	Yugoslavia	1,782	600
	Zaire	58	
1984	Brazil	15,200	6,500
	Chile	1,200	780
	Ecuador	500	
	Guyana	42	
	Jamaica	165	
	Madagascar	195	
	Mexico	–	3,800
	Nicaragua	145	
	Niger	27	
	Poland	1,950	750
	Senegal	92	
	Sierra Leone	25	
	Sudan	838	
	Yugoslavia	1,268	
	Zaire	64	
	Zambia	74	

Table 1.1. – cont.

Year	Debtor countries	Amounts restructured (in US$ million)	New money
1985	Argentina	16,800	4,200
	Chile	7,640	1,085
	Costa Rica	532	75
	Cuba	580	
	Ecuador	2,473	200
	Ivory Coast	500	104
	Jamaica	396	
	Mexico	49,650	
	Panama	796	60
	Philippines	8,860	925
	Senegal	23	
	Sudan	800	
	Yugoslavia	3,800	
	Zaire	61	
1986	Argentina	10,000	
	Brazil	35,800	
	Dominican Republic	787	
	Ecuador	2,487	220
	Ivory Coast	691	
	Mexico	950	500
	Morocco	538	750
	Poland	3,600	
	Romania	880	
	Uruguay	–	90
	Venezuela	21,088	
	Zaire	65	
1987 (till 7/87)	Argentina	32,449	1,950
	Chile	14,190	
	Gabon	70	
	Ecuador	135	
	Mexico	52,250	7,700
	Morocco	1,725	
	Panama	421	
	Philippines	11,457	
	South Africa	13,000	

Sources: 'Recent Development in External Debt Restructuring', Occasional Paper No. 40, International Monetary Fund, Washington DC, October 1985, as well as other sources.

Europe, it managed many issues in the nineteenth century that enabled the construction of the railway networks in Austria and France. It also placed issues for Spanish mining companies.

Since the mid-nineteenth century, however, banks with publicly issued capital have increasingly become the important intermediaries in international financing. As a result, most aspects of international banking, such as classic commercial international banking, export financing, correspondent banking and foreign exchange – as well as international bond and share issues – were all known activities of the major banks at the end of the last century. J. P. Morgan was one of the tycoons of that time, which is reflected in the names of three very prestigious financial institutions. In those days banks also started their first branches and subsidiaries abroad; many had followed the colonialisation efforts of their governments. The scale of lending involved and the instruments used were different from today. International lending was short-term commercial lending. Long-term financing was done through bond and share issues. Small investors from Europe lost considerable amounts of money through investments in bonds and shares of foreign borrowers, mainly railway and mining companies. Part of the infrastructure of quite a few countries in Europe and North America was financed in such a way. This should not be forgotten when we look at the financial difficulties of some of the less-developed countries (LDCs) of today.

The international lending we talk about today is, however, a result of the growth of the Euromarket – a phenomenon of the 1960s. A Euromarket transaction is a transaction where the borrower takes up a loan in a financial centre in a currency other than the one used for domestic transactions in that financial centre. The first such transactions were made by the East European countries with London banks in order to avoid placing their foreign currency reserves at that time, mainly US dollars, in the United States. Other events that helped to develop the Euromarket were the minimum reserve requirements in the United States, the famous regulation Q,[1] and other restrictions on the free flow of international capital. The first users of the Euromarket were the expanding overseas subsidiaries of large US corporations. In those early days, bond issues were as prominent as Eurocredits. This is one of the reasons why country risk exposures by banks were not yet of major significance.

The next boost to the Euromarket was given on the supply side by the 1973 hike in oil prices. The major international banks were suddenly faced with a big recycling task for all the OPEC money looking for a return on investment. Coincidentally, by the early 1970s a rapid growth period had

---

1. Regulation Q is a regulation of the Board of Governors of the Federal Reserve System and deals with the interest on deposits. It has been amended several times and some parts of it are still valid, but do not concern international lending.

started in many LDCs. Previous financing schemes through official aid could not keep pace with that growth so that these countries began to tap the emerging Eurocurrency credit market more and more. This enabled the LDCs to take up funds without policy requirements and recommendations. Banks were eager to accept these new borrowers, since the 1973–74 recession had substantially reduced the borrowing requirements of companies in the developed world. As LDCs shifted their borrowing from concessional to non-concessional funding, they were suddenly exposed to higher interest rates and shorter maturities than had been the case with traditional sources of development aid. By 1978, the 1973 oil price increase had been digested by many countries and the current account status of most industrialised and developing countries was back where it had been in 1973. The relatively modest interest rates, inflation and the substantial depreciation of the US dollar had helped that adjustment process.

The second oil shock, in 1979, had far greater consequences than the first one. Recycling proved much more difficult and risky. The world economy plunged into a recession from which it began to recover only in 1983. Monetary policies in the United States raised interest rates to historically high levels. For the first time, the recession in many industrialised countries showed structural deficiencies and produced an ever-increasing rate of unemployment. Nevertheless, many countries still believed they could master the second oil shock as well as they had the first one and did not adjust their economic policies accordingly. Oil-rich LDCs even began to believe that rising oil prices would bring them the wealth of industrialised nations and, therefore, adopted highly expansionary policies. Trade and current account balances in most oil-importing countries turned heavily into the red. The financing of budget deficits (and not only investment projects and trade deficits) became a new feature of the Eurocurrency market. Table 1.2 shows the development of the Euromarket since 1970.

The funding of all these financing needs was made possible through several coincidental developments. As already mentioned, the huge new OPEC funds were looking for a return. The profitability of international lending in the early 1970s had prompted many medium-sized and regional banks to become engaged in international lending by participating in Euro-syndicated credits. Many new banks established branches or subsidiaries in the London market, which became the turntable for Eurolending. Consortium banks were founded to take care of specific lending propositions.

Luxembourg established itself as a Eurolending base for mainly West German and Scandinavian banks. Hong Kong and Singapore followed. Table 1.3 shows the increase in banking presence in London, Luxembourg, Hong Kong and Singapore since 1970. These developments have led to the fact that the largest proportion of current cross-border debt has its origin in

Table 1.2. Bonds issued and published medium-term Eurocurrency credits (US$ billion)

	1975	1976	1977	1978	1979	1980	1981	1982	1983	1984	1985	1986
International bond issues	20.0	32.5	34.0	34.3	40.9	41.9	53.0	78.0	75.7	107.4	167.8	226.4
Year-on-year % change	194.1	62.5	4.6	0.9	19.2	2.4	26.5	47.2	-3.0	41.8	56.2	34.9
– Eurobonds	8.6	14.3	17.8	14.1	18.7	24.0	31.6	51.6	48.5	79.5	136.7	188.0
Year-on-year % change	309.5	66.3	24.4	-20.8	32.6	28.3	31.7	63.3	-6.0	63.9	71.9	37.5
– Foreign bonds	11.4	18.2	16.2	20.2	22.2	17.9	21.4	26.4	27.2	28.0	31.0	38.4
Year-on-year % change	142.6	59.6	-11.0	24.7	9.9	-19.4	19.5	23.3	3.0	3.0	10.7	23.9
– Outside US	4.9	7.6	8.8	14.4	17.7	14.5	13.8	20.5	22.8	22.5	26.3	32.3
Year-on-year % change	250.0	55.1	15.8	63.6	22.9	-18.1	-4.8	48.5	11.2	-1.3	16.9	22.8
– Inside US	6.5	10.6	7.4	5.8	4.5	3.4	7.6	5.9	4.4	5.5	4.7	6.1
Year-on-year % change	97.0	63.1	-30.2	-21.6	-22.4	-24.4	123.5	-22.4	-25.4	25.0	-14.5	29.8
Eurocredits	21.0	28.8	41.8	70.2	82.8	77.4	133.4	84.9	73.9	112.6	110.3	82.7
Year-on-year % change	-28.4	37.1	45.1	67.9	17.9	-6.5	72.3	-36.4	-13.0	52.4	-2.0	-25.0

Source: World Financial Markets, Morgan Guaranty Trust, New York.

Definitions for Table 1.2

An international bond issue is one sold outside the country of the borrower. It may be either a Eurobond issue or a foreign bond issue.

A Eurobond issue is one underwritten by an international syndicate and sold principally in countries other than the country of the currency in which the issue is denominated.

A foreign bond issue is one underwritten by a syndicate composed of members from one country, sold principally in that country and denominated in the currency of that country, for a borrower of another country.

A Eurocredit is a loan in a currency which is not native to the country in which the bank office making the loan is located.

Data on new international bond issue volume include all publicly announced issues with an original maturity of three years or more, whether publicly or privately placed, but exclude those where the investor is a central bank, monetary authority or government.

Data on new Eurocurrency bank credit volume include all publicly announced loans with an original maturity of one year or more. A loan is included in the period in which the lending banks make a commitment covering the amount and terms of the loan to the borrowers.

Table 1.3. Development of foreign bank presence in London, Luxembourg, Singapore and Hong Kong

	London* directly[1]	London* indirectly[2]	Luxembourg**[3]	Singapore	Hong Kong[4]
1970	163	—	23	26	50
1971	176	25	29	31	79
1972	215	28	37	33	84
1973	232	35	56	43	90
1974	264	72	63	50	106
1975	263	72	64	57	120
1976	265	78	66	59	133
1977	300	55	78	64	140
1978	313	69	85	68	159
1979	330	59	96	76	185
1980	353	50	99	84	186
1981	353	65	102	105	210
1982	379	70	102	106	211
1983	391	69	102	108	237
1984	403	67	103	116	238
1985	399	64	117	122	276
1986	400	47	122	129	281

1. Representative offices, branches, subsidiaries.
2. Representation through a stake in a joint venture or consortium bank.
3. Excluded are Belgian banks.
4. Representative offices, subsidiaries, licensed deposit-taking companies.
* *The Banker*, November 1986.
** *Bulletin trimestriel de l'Institut Monétaire Luxembourgeois.*

the Euromarket. Government-guaranteed lending and lending by the supranational institutions are the other two major sources of cross-border lending today.

Critical voices regarding the development of the Euromarket have been raised for many years. They have not changed the market, but have certainly had an influence on the development of some of the tools dealt with in this book. The first lightning struck the Euromarket with the Polish crisis of August 1981. The Falkland Islands conflict was the forerunner of earthquakes that Mexico and Brazil produced in the market for international lending. Rescheduling of international debts has by now become a task for nearly all banks with cross-border exposures. However, the number, the pace and the amounts have increased dramatically.

2

Country risk versus credit risk

Every lending involves a credit risk, i.e. the risk that the borrower will not be able to pay interest on his loan and repay the principal when it becomes due. We can call this the solvency risk. In order to minimise that risk, lending has developed sophisticated methods and appraisals to evaluate the borrower's capability of honouring his debts. The bank as a typical lending institution is, therefore, very interested in the economic status of the borrower and analyses it carefully. Not only is past performance reviewed; forecasts of future development are of even greater importance. The lending officer wants to know what the loan is to be used for and out of which cash flow the interest and redemption of principal will be paid. Another question he will certainly ask the borrower is when the loan will be repaid. In many cases the lender will ask for collateral to further diminish his credit risk in view of the difficulty in evaluating his customer's future economic performance. If the risk should materalise, the lender has in most cases the possibility of taking legal action against the borrower, who is also bound to follow the legal procedure undertaken against him.

In cross-border lending some additional components to the credit risk have to be evaluated and dealt with. They can be summarised under what is defined as country risk, i.e. the aspects beyond the usual risks which arise in relation to all lending.

Cross-border transactions always involve a foreign currency risk. It can be a foreign currency risk for the borrower only, for the lender only, or for both. A British bank confirming a letter of credit of a Brazilian bank in US dollars involves a foreign currency risk for both parties. A Luxembourg consortium bank lending Deutschmarks to a West German company means a foreign currency risk for the lender only. A US bank lending US dollars to a Japanese company is a typical foreign currency risk for the borrower. When we talk about foreign currency risk as part of the country risk, we mean the foreign currency risk that the borrower runs. This risk is basically twofold. One risk stems from parity adjustments, obligating the borrower to pay a substantially different amount in local currency than was due when he contracted his obligation. This can impair his solvency considerably, as was recently shown by lendings to the private sector in Mexico. The other risk is that at the time of payment the borrower cannot remit the foreign currency because the authorities of his country have introduced corresponding foreign currency remittance regulations – 'corresponding' in that they relate to the borrower's liability in foreign currencies. In both cases the lender is faced with a country risk problem which has its origin in the economic policies of that country. Very often the lender will have to agree to the rescheduling of the debt in one way or another.

Another factor that can be associated with country risk is the difficulty of dialogue between lender and borrower. The further a borrower is situated from a lender, the more probable it is that the dialogue will be difficult due to language problems, cultural differences or even time zones.

Cross-border transactions also entail a higher legal risk because the laws of more than one country are involved. In order to minimise the potential problems for both partners, the choice of legal form is usually the choice of the law of a certain country. In this connection English law has become very popular in international lending. The recommendations of the International Chamber of Commerce in Paris are the basis of most transactions in the field of documentary credits and collections. Legal risk can become especially evident if the partner of the bank does not fulfil his obligations and the bank has to sue him in his country of domicile. The sovereign risk can manifest itself as a typical case of legal risk.

Political risk is usually associated with political turmoil and revolution. Embargo or boycott measures instituted for whatever reason can lead to solvency problems for the borrower since he might, for example, no longer be in a position to run his company. They can also mean a substantial change in the foreign currency reserve position of a country. Labour unrest and nationalisation are other incidents through which political risk and, therefore, country risk, can spell problems for a lending institution. Syndication risk is one of the more recent aspects of political risk. The well-known case of the freezing of Iranian assets by the United States in 1981 and, therefore, the inability of Iran to fulfil its US dollar debts to non-US banks, has been a typical case history of a syndication risk.

Looking at all these risks, it seems that the appraisal of country risk as a factor in cross-border transactions is very complex, therefore making cross-border lending much more difficult than domestic lending. It is worth going into detail briefly here to enumerate some of the influences on solvency or credit risk, in order to show that for credit risk, too, a multitude of factors must be evaluated. In credit risk analyses the lending officer must have intimate knowledge of the markets in which his client operates. He must appraise the production know-how and technology of his client. Quality of management is another factor to be evaluated. However, he always has an audited statement of the financial status of his client, something that is clearly missing in country risk assessment.

We may, therefore, say that country risk, like credit risk, is influenced by many different factors. However, it is probably easier to evaluate and quantify credit risk than country risk since the influencing factors can be better appraised.

In a transaction that involves a country risk we will always have a credit risk as well. Country risk usually manifests itself separately from credit risk, with the exception of the transaction that involves a sovereign risk. The credit risk can, therefore, cause no problems as the creditor is fully solvent, while the country risk has become an apparent risk. This is often the situation of private debt in a rescheduling operation.

Credit risk in its most extreme form is the bankruptcy of the debtor. In this situation the lender participates in the bankruptcy proceedings, either recuperating part of his credit or losing it completely, thus having to write off the credit as a total loss.

Country risk manifests itself in three different ways, each one being an aggravation of the previous one. The lightest consequence of a country risk that materialises is a delay in the payment of interest or in the repayment of principal. This kind of problem is either of a rather minor significance or can be the beginning of a more serious problem for the country involved. It can also mean that the country allocates its foreign exchange partially by discriminating against private companies and using it all for the sovereign debt. A delay in payment was mostly a technical matter in the 1970s and Eurobankers have therefore been familiar with it. It was considered a temporary weakness of the borrower, without any further consequences. Since the wave of reschedulings started, however, delay in payment has assumed much greater significance and today usually means the first sign of serious difficulties for the country in question. For this reason, delays in payments due should be communicated immediately to the persons or units within an organisation who are responsible for that country.

The next step in the deterioration of a country risk is a lasting weakness of the country in honouring its debts and in making the necessary foreign exchange available to resident cross-border borrowers. In this case the situation is already much more worrisome as the country can no longer pay interest or repay the principal due on its public and private foreign debt.

The country involved has two options: either renegotiate and reschedule its debts or declare a moratorium.

In such a situation, the option of renegotiation or rescheduling is usually chosen these days. The debtor country and the lenders renegotiate the existing debt in order to adapt it better to the country's ability to service its foreign debts. An extension is usually granted for repayment of the principal. The spreads are often readjusted, with additional lending to help the country involved to adjust its economy.

However, if a country declares a moratorium for its debt, it simply stops servicing its debts with the understanding that as soon as it has adjusted its external situation it will again do so. The choice of a moratorium has not been popular so far as it overemphasizes the relationship between borrower and lender. It therefore also makes it much more difficult for the borrowing country to have renewed access to financial markets. Cynics may say that there is not much difference between a renegotiation or rescheduling and a moratorium. One might not completely disagree with that, considering the way in which some of the 1983 reschedulings were introduced to the international banking community. At the same time we never had the legal characteristics of a moratorium. This has now changed.

The most severe consequence of a country risk that materialises occurs when a country repudiates its debts. The country will refuse to honour its debts on the grounds that it no longer accepts them. This is, however, an exceptional situation, because in so doing the specific country isolates itself completely from the international financial and economic community. The latest case of repudiation was in the 1960s, when Cuba repudiated the debt it had incurred with US lenders. The USSR repudiated its debt after the Revolution and many savers lost substantial amounts of money on their Russian bonds.

These direct damages arising for the lender or lenders out of country risk usually generate indirect damages or negative consequences. The traffic of goods, capital and payments between the debtor country and the outside may be impaired. The credit risk of the private sector of the country involved will deteriorate. Cross-default clauses can involve other borrowers and/or other lenders. Repercussions can be felt by countries not directly involved, as has been shown by the difficulties some Comecon countries encountered when they operated on international markets at the height of the Polish crisis.

Only in very rare cases so far has country risk meant for the lender the same as bankruptcy in the context of credit risk. This is understandable given that countries by definition cannot go bankrupt. It has, however, led to changes and adjustments in the relation between lender and borrower. These changes and adjustments would not have been necessary in view of the evaluation of only the credit risk involved.

3

The heterogeneous club of countries

While the definition of country risk as outlined above is largely accepted, we have to bear in mind that the term 'country' carries a host of different meanings. Just as commercial debtors have different products, different financial strengths and different managements, we find that the same is true of countries. It therefore might be useful to group countries into specific categories as companies are grouped into specific industries.

We have, for example, the steel industry, the automobile companies, the electronics and highly technical sectors, the insurance industry and so on. Within each of these industries, companies have certain things in common, but they also have a clearly different status as possible borrowers of funds. We will always find above-average, average and below-average performers in the same industry. The whole industry, however, often performs according to a specific pattern and trend that cannot be influenced by any one company.

Prudent banking looks for a diversification of risks. It will, therefore, structure its lending portfolio by diversifying into different industries, then trying to pick the best credit risks in each. Similar ideas can be followed when we look at countries. The question is then what kind of classification we should seek for the heterogeneous club of countries. Should we look at the geographical pattern and talk about the Latin American countries or the African countries, or should we try another classification? It would seem that we have today five main types of countries, which follow broadly the World Bank classification. Countries themselves can move from type to type over a certain period of time. However, the change from one group of countries to another comes only gradually and usually very slowly. These five types of countries are the main industrial nations, the smaller industrialised countries, the countries with a state-planned economy, the newly industrialised countries and the less-developed countries (LDCs). This structure seems to focus in a useful direction when we have to assess country risk and is, therefore, more helpful than the geographical pattern. It takes into account the economic development of a country, which is often synonymous with its financial strength.

Main industrial nations

This group consists of the major industrial countries of Europe and North America, as well as Japan. They are the main political and economic powers and pillars of the Western world. They have a well-diversified, high-quality industrial base and a substantial home market. Their exports are important, but usually not greater than 25 per cent of gross national product (GNP) – which is higher than US$300 billion. Population in general exceeds 50 million inhabitants per country. Currencies are fully convertible and capital market transactions are fairly liberal. Large differences exist only in the amount and diversification of natural resources.

Smaller industrialised countries

These include all the other West European countries as well as Australia and New Zealand. Within this group of countries we already have a much wider spectrum. In size they range from Australia's 7,682,000 square km to the Netherlands' 41,160 square km, in population from Spain's 37.8 million to Norway's 4.1 million, and in GNP per head from Switzerland's US$20,437 to Portugal's US$2,650. What they all have in common is a political system based on democratic principles. For all of them foreign trade is of prime importance in order to balance their vital imports. Infrastructure is well developed.

Countries with a state-planned economy

This third category encompasses all the Comecon countries. These had been considered as being a bloc supported politically and economically by the Soviet Union. In this context the so-called umbrella theory was propounded, meaning that the Soviet Union would cover its allies by an umbrella against all kinds of difficulty they might face, mainly in the economic sector. Events in Poland and Romania have, however, shown that this theory was highly speculative. All Comecon countries obviously have in common their political system, based on one-party rule. They plan their economies through a central institution, usually on a five-year basis. This, however, should not prevent us from seeing the substantially different profiles of these countries, ranging from the island of Cuba to the continental state of Mongolia and from subtropical Vietnam to the highly industrialised German Democratic Republic.

Newly industrialised countries

Since the 1960s, these countries have developed an industrial base capable of competing on international markets. They have different political systems. The tooling up to a modern industrialised state, however, was possible only through substantial imports of capital goods, which forced these countries into heavy foreign borrowing. They are, therefore – in absolute and relative terms – high up on the list of countries with foreign debts. The newly industrialised countries depend very much for their well-being on the development of world trade.

LDCs

This last group of countries is by far the largest by geographical extension and population. (Less developed in this context means in comparison with the economies of the OECD countries.) These countries represent a wide range of political and economic systems and are extremely varied in size and population. However, they can probably be divided quite adequately into two categories: those that produce oil, and all the others.

It is sensible to make this distinction because the countries with oil as a natural resource have a substantial foreign exchange source which all the others lack. This foreign exchange source will remain of importance in quantity as well as quality, certainly until the end of this century, owing to the dependence of the world economy on oil. However, the price variations of the past few years have shown that too much dependence on oil can be a mixed blessing. Most oil-producing countries have grouped themselves in the Organization of Petroleum Exporting Countries (OPEC), which represents their common interests. Within OPEC we have the low-absorbing countries (such as Saudi Arabia) and the high-absorbing countries (e.g. Nigeria and Iran). The latter countries use the earned foreign exchange to a great extent due to their large and fast-growing populations, whereas in the former, the ratio of wealth from resources to the relatively small populations is very significant.

The non-oil-producing LDCs constitute a category that is easily defined. It is, however, the category of countries comprising the greatest differences. These differences are relevant in nearly every parameter – e.g. population, political system, geographical size, economic development and natural resources. This must be borne in mind when we talk about non-oil-producing LDCs.

It might be asked why a general classification into five groups is made when there are such big differences among the various countries. The major reason lies in the context of country analysis; the countries in each group have similarities that allow a useful comparison which can then lead to sensible conclusions. In addition, the statistical data available for each group have a similar qualitative standard.

Sources of data

Data on which to base the appraisal of a country are available from a diversity of sources. However, their qualitative and quantitative character-istics vary widely. In addition, the majority of data available are historical and, therefore, not of too great value for forecasting the future. And these data are usually available only after a substantial time lag. Of the different sources of data, those collected by the International Monetary Fund (IMF), the World Bank and the Bank for International Settlements (BIS) are certainly the most reliable. They cover most member states of the International Monetary Fund as well as Switzerland and the Netherlands Antilles, which means the great majority of all countries. The Institute of International Finance, Inc. has become a further important source of data.

International Financial Statistics is a monthly publication of the International Monetary Fund. It takes into account all major aspects of international and domestic finance of the countries covered and is presented through country pages, tables of areas and world aggregates. The country pages show major economic aggregates used in the analysis of economic developments and generally include data on the country's exchange rates, international liquidity, money and banking, government accounts, production, prices, international transactions and national accounts. The sources of data quoted are usually published by the central bank as well as by the national institute of statistics of the country involved. Whereas some data are fairly recent, other important data can be rather old. For example, in the issue of June 1987 export data were available as follows: Mexico January 1987, Brazil February 1987, Yugoslavia December 1986 and Sweden April 1987. In the same issue balance-of-payments data were available for Romania for the second quarter 1986, Argentina for the second quarter 1986, Nigeria for 1985 and Denmark for the fourth quarter 1986.

The International Monetary Fund also publishes monthly balance-of-payments and direction-of-trade statistics. Furthermore, a year-book is published from *International Financial Statistics* covering available annual data for 30 years, as well as the year-book *Government Finance Statistics Year Book*, which provides data on all the major parameters of government finances. It contains information from 124 countries with data up to the previous ten years.

The statistics available from the IMF are, from the qualitative point of view, certainly the best, bearing in mind that the quality of the data delivered by different countries does vary. However, the tables give no explanation of the published figures.

The world debt tables of the World Bank are another valuable source of information, as they show external debt of over 100 reporting countries. External debt is defined as debt owed to non-residents and repayable in foreign currency, goods or services, with an original or extended maturity of over one year. A distinction is then made between public debt, publicly guaranteed debt and private non-guaranteed debt. Excluded are transactions with the International Monetary Fund – with the exception of trust fund loans, debts repayable in local currency, direct investments and short-term debts. Not all countries reporting account for private non-guaranteed debt. Besides the debt figures the tables show some interesting ratios, including the debt service ratio (i.e. total debt service to exports of goods and all services) and the interest service ratio (i.e. interest payments to exports of goods and all services). In addition, for outstanding and disbursed public debt, the portion that is on concessional terms is mentioned as well as the portion that carries variable interest rates.

The way of reporting is being reviewed. The world debt tables cover the last eight years and also show projected public debt service for the coming eight years. The same is done with private non-guaranteed debt for the countries that report on that aspect. The world debt tables are also a very valuable instrument in appraising a country's external situation. However, a major time lag exists between figures and publication date, and short-term debt is not covered.

The OECD countries' economies are reviewed annually by the OECD, with a report then published for each country reviewed. The country reports are based on the assumptions made by the respective ministries of finance, trade and/or economics. The reports contain a lot of text with the statistical information and are, therefore, easily understandable. For OECD countries these reports form one of the prime sources of country information. In addition, the OECD publishes data on certain topics.

Comecon countries are not covered by the International Monetary Fund,[1] the World Bank or the OECD. Comecon publishes a year-book, but since it is published in Russian, it is difficult to read for the average country specialist. Furthermore, terminology is different from that used outside Comecon. A comparison on the same trade data from Western and Eastern sources therefore shows discrepancies which are difficult to reconcile. For some economic indicators only changes in percentage points are given, with the basis missing. Sometimes even the basis is changed, and at fairly frequent intervals. The foreign debt aspect is not covered at all. Consequently, outside sources must be relied on to appraise the Comecon countries.

1. With the exception of Hungary, Poland and Romania.

The Vienna Institute for Comparative Economic Studies has for many years analysed the Comecon countries and evaluated their economic data. It can, therefore, be considered an authority on Comecon and one of the best sources of Comecon data. Regular statistical data are published in the biennial series Comecon Data and in Comecon Foreign Trade Data. However, most data are of historical value only since they are published with a certain time lag.

Other sources of data are the statistical services of the United Nations and its different agencies. In addition, several private organisations publish data. Their sources are, however, usually the ones indicated above. The major problem with statistical data will always be accuracy and speed. It is hoped that further advances in computer technology will be able to alleviate this problem. For the time being, we have to live with a fairly heterogeneous bunch of statistical data and figures.

Part Two

Assessment of country risk

4

General aspects

As already mentioned, country risk consists of two separate risks – political risk and transfer risk. Political risk involves the will to honour one's obligations, whereas transfer risk depends on the capability to honour one's debt. Both these risks, however, do interrelate. They probably do not depend completely on each other, but very often are mutually influential. This is especially the case if one of the two risks is worsening. The other risk is then frequently drawn along. An example is the situation where the economy of a country has suffered substantially due to changes – e.g. in international commodity prices such as copper – which then leads to enhanced political instability due to economic difficulties. This instability obviously brings with it a worsening of political risk. Transfer risk can also be very much influenced by political decisions; the most obvious example is Comecon, where it is difficult to separate the two risks.

The interrelation of the two types of risk is, nevertheless, difficult to qualify. In the overall *assessment* of country risk, the interrelation of the two risks will become manifest through weighing them both. In the *analysis* of country risk the two elements should be dealt with separately. It is, therefore, advisable to evaluate each risk separately in order to find out its characteristics.

5

The political element:
the will to honour obligations

Assessment of political risk – the political element or the will to honour
one's obligations – is one of the two elements to be assessed when we
evaluate country risk. It is essential at the very beginning to make a clear
distinction between 'political instability' and 'political risk'. The former
can exist and not endanger our business interests. It is usually unmeasured
and, to some extent, subjective. We are more interested in assessing the
latter, political risk. To do so we need some sort of system by which the use
of political 'intelligence' can identify the degree of political instability and
go on to assess the degree of risk; this then is usually a standardised
measure.

When trying to find out what factors constitute political risk, it is
essential to bear in mind that different types of organisation are likely to
have quite specific needs. So while there is undoubtedly a 'best' system for
each organisation, there is unlikely to be a 'best' system as such. However, a
common framework will serve to systematise what are, in essence,
subjective judgements. There are a number of factors which will always
have to be taken into account, regardless of the type of business being done.

Political risk factors

A crucial factor to be taken into consideration in any political evaluation is
the role of actors. Individuals, groups of individuals or other countries are
all actors, for example, a Minister of Finance, the Roman Catholic Church
and the Soviet Union can all, in one country or other, be considered key
actors. Actors play a central role in, or strongly influence, a country's
political situation, or they play a key role in certain issues. Actors will tend

to have more individual importance in less developed countries than in the industrialised West – take, for example, the key role played in the Philippines in early 1986 by the Roman Catholic Church.

Other political risk factors can either be inherent in, evolve out of, or have their origins outside a particular country. The political risk factors that come from within a country can evolve within the constitutional proceedings or outside that framework. These factors can have a positive or negative influence on the degree of political risk in the country involved. Political events create not only risks but also opportunities. Within each of the categories given below the key actors must be identified. We must also assess their intentions and their capabilities. The more we know about a key actor and about the political relationship between key actors, the more we are able to assess the political situation in a given country.

Political risk factors inherent in a country

Constitutional environment

A constitution incorporating the basic principles of Western democratic thinking provides the framework for political stability for a country's institutions. The important question here is whether a constitution as written is actually enforced. Failure, for example, on the part of a government to ensure people their constitutional rights will sow the seed of resentment and discontent and thus potential political instability. Equally, an ambiguous interpretation of a country's constitution by the government must raise doubts about that government's credibility.

It is also important to establish whether the constitution provides the framework within which a government must act – thus protecting the rights of all citizens; or whether governments use the constitution as an instrument to achieve their own ends. Here it is useful to examine how often a constitution has been revised in a given country.

Political parties

The nature of these and the type of programme offered can have a major bearing on political risk. The significance of political parties is often out of all proportion to their size as, for example, when a small party regularly holds the balance of power, and is thus regularly in government (in coalition). The one-party system can be a factor of stability or the major factor of instability, depending on whether parties are system- or personality-oriented. The former is the case in communist countries, the latter in many developing countries. A balanced party system that provides a strong government as well as an accepted opposition usually provides the basis for political stability. However, very often parties are not allowed to function as is the custom in a really democratic-system. It is further worth

27

remembering the influence of political parties in exile or of political figures who would, under other circumstances, lead a political party in their own country. The existence of such parties or personalities can affect the policies and actions of government and opposition, for example, the African National Congress (ANC), of South Africa.

Quality of government

This is another major factor in assessing political risk. Can the government act or is it blocked by the influence of pressure groups? In this connection it is essential to check the quality of the bureaucracy of a country because the bureaucracy is often even more important than the government, especially in the day-to-day running of the country. In many countries the bureaucracy becomes itself a major actor, largely because of its ability, by its actions or by inaction, to affect government policy. The major part of an administration normally does not change with the government. Only top-echelon members of an administration are changed if they are politically appointed. The four-year election modus in many countries prevents drastic changes by members of government in the way a bureaucracy operates, because the time span is too short to implement effective change. Nevertheless, a change of government always has an influence on the degree of political risk, not because a change of government by election is a destabilising factor *per se*, but because it usually brings change. (This change need not necessarily be welcomed by the country's business partners!)

Government crises

The importance of government crises for political risk is two-fold: one, the obvious danger of serious instability, and the possibility of solution by *coup d'état*; and two, the danger of government paralysis resulting in party political negotiations to find common ground, rather than effective government.

Foreign policy

The adherence of a given country to one or other major bloc or the group of the neutral and non-aligned countries is an important factor in the evaluation of political risk inasmuch as it tells which Third World countries might exert an influence on the internal affairs of that country, and to what extent. Equally, a country's foreign policy changes, usually a result of a change in government, can have far-reaching effects both on internal stability and on the government's dealings with Third World countries (for example, Egypt's turn to the West under President Sadat, and the uncertainty over the future of the US bases in the Philippines under

President Aquino). Furthermore, a country's strategic position has a definitive influence on its foreign policy.

Economic systems

The functioning of a government's economic policies within a given economic system can affect the political situation and thus the degree of political risk. Obvious examples are the policies of certain Latin American governments that resulted in serious foreign debt problems. This means that a government might have to take tough political decisions which can also affect foreign investment. The size of the state-controlled sector of the economy has its importance for it can be assumed that a growing state-controlled sector might hinder the environment for private initiative and therefore provide a potential political risk.

Social structures

These constitute a major political factor influencing the stability of a country. Considerable inequality, either between urban and rural populations or between different layers of the population, is a source of conflict. Social inqualities are frequently linked with government crises (paralysis), high debt problems, outright instability or violence, and ethnic, racial or religious problems. Equal distribution of wealth and jobs will go a long way to reduce potential political risk in the social structure of any country. The literacy rate is also part of the social structure. The literacy rate of a country must, however, be taken together with other factors if we are to evaluate its significance for political stability. For example, oversimplified, we might say the following:

> high literacy rate
>   *and*   = discontent − instability
> unequal distribution of income
>   *or*
> high literacy rate
>   *and*   = contentment − stability
> equal distribution of income
>   *but also*
> low literacy rate
>   *and*   = lack of awareness − stability
> unequal distribution of income

Demographic structure

Considerable urban migration creates overcrowding, bad housing and other infrastructural problems which lead to crime, violence and social difficulties. There is an obvious danger of political instability here which could lead to political risk. In addition, if there has been high urban migration there is a danger that a government will concentrate resources in the cities and neglect rural areas where very often traditional sectors of the economy are concentrated. These deteriorate, leading to social and political problems and political resentment. The trend towards urban migration occurs most often in developing countries where opportunity is associated with urban rather than agricultural areas. Also, a population dependent on industry and services will have quite different political ambitions than those of a largely agricultural society.

Ethnic and religious differences

Countries vary substantially in their ethnic and religious composition and the existence of one or more minority, ethnic or religious group can provide the basis for political instability, particularly if, for example, this group perceives that the government is discriminating against it, or it is excluded from the political process, or it is pursuing separatist claims. Ethnic and religious differences become especially explosive if differences of wealth and population are superimposed. The Kurds in Turkey are a constant nuisance factor for the government owing to their terrorist attacks on persons and installations. Lebanon is another example of a country where internal tensions are due to religious and ethnic differences.

Labour relations

The quality of Labour relations can also be classified as a political risk factor, particularly where unions are a substantial political force, or where they are very closely connected with a political party. The militancy or political involvement of unions can have a direct bearing on political stability. Analysis of labour relations and review of labour-related legislation is thus necessary when appraising political risk in a country.

Legislation regarding foreign investment

This will be a direct reflection of government policy towards foreign investment, therefore, it will be of the first importance to be aware of government policy on this issue, and of the views of major government and opposition actors, so that possible changes in legislation, or indeed in government policy not enshrined in legislation, can be anticipated in good time.

Political risk factors resulting from the above factors

Internal turmoil

This is usually the expression of dissatisfaction caused by any of the aforementioned factors – for example, ethnic or religious problems, labour

30

militancy or social inequalities. This is a major factor in domestic instability and usually carries a high degree of political risk. Separatism, for example, can lead to turmoil and can even culminate in the break-up of countries, for example, the creation of Bangladesh. The religious, linguistic and social differences between the Walloons and the Flemings in Belgium provide a good example of a situation with the potential for internal turmoil.

Rebellious conflicts

These will destabilise any country. In its most extreme form rebellious conflict leads to civil war. Such conflicts obviously increase political risk. Examples are the Spanish Civil War in the 1930s, the Biafra War, and the war in El Salvador.

Revolution or coup d'état

These events are the ultimate threat to any government. Very often they change not only the political structure, but also the social and economic structure. But both revolutions (for example, the Philippines in early 1986) and *coups d'état* (Turkey 1980) can be welcomed in the country concerned, and can usher in an improved political situation. It can also come to pass, however, that a revolution or a *coup d'état* welcomed by the people of a country can be detrimental to business transactions entered into with the government overthrown. Thus we can see the importance of assessing the intentions and the capabilities of major actors in the country who might lead a revolution or a *coup d'état*. Iran is the most prominent recent example of a revolution.

Corruption

This is yet another political risk factor. As such, however, it can vary substantially from country to country in its significance. It can be part of the way of life in a country. It can, therefore, go as far as becoming the deciding factor in obtaining certain behaviour from the institutions of a specific country. Corruption is not *per se* a destabilising political factor but its implications for the institutions of the country in question need attention. Corruption can be used to further enrich just a few or it can be the basis of income of the whole underpaid administration.

Political risk factors having their origin outside the specific country
Non-belligerent intervention

Such intervention by a third country can appear in the form of subversion. It can also take the form of internal turmoil or even rebellious conflicts through economic help or deliveries of weapons. Lebanon and Central America are areas where third countries have intervened in this way.

Discriminating acts

This sort of pressure can be applied by Third World countries or by international organisations and, in some circumstances, by multi-national corporations (for example, disinvestment in South Africa). To some extent, this political risk factor has its origins within the specific country, for it will be as a result of government policies, or of circumstances within the country, that these acts of discrimination will be performed (for example, South Africa again).

War or warlike conflicts

These can occur directly between two countries, but can also develop into multilateral conflicts where several countries are involved. Open multilateral conflicts and wars have fortunately become rare since the Second World War. Today warlike conflicts are very often frontier conflicts, of which there have been many since 1945. If they have taken place in one specific country they have always changed the quality of political risk for the countries involved, because the political institutions are absorbed by the conflict. Furthermore, such conflicts devour enormous sums of money and produce substantial economic strain. At the time of writing, there are more than five such situations world-wide, an important one being the conflict between Iraq and Iran.

Assessment of political risk

While identification of the different political risk factors is relatively easy, their asssment is much more difficult. Originally, the need and justification for the assessment was mainly to foresee the risk of expropriation for political reasons, e.g. revolution. Today, however, the assessment of political risk is not only the task of foreseeing a deteriorating situation; it is equally important to find new opportunities where the degree of political risk is diminishing. Political analysis can usually discover opportunities at an earlier stage than economic indicators can.

In assessing political risk one finds basically three different approaches: the qualitative, the quantitative, and an integrated one. The qualitative approach focuses on the experience of experts who have the knowledge and analytical ability to assess the different political risk factors. The quantitative method gives a numerical value to the different political factors enumerated and then tries to predict the political risk by using a multivariate analysis. The integrated approach combines both methods.

Whatever the system, the assessment has to be systematic in order to be worth while. It must take place at regular intervals, using the same methods. It is further necessary to make an individual assessment after a major political event has occurred, or even better to forecast such an event in time and make a corresponding assessment. Assessment of political risk factors can lead to a classification of the different countries according to the scale of:

– extremely high risk
– high risk
– medium risk
– low risk
– very low risk

Instead of a verbal scale one can obviously use a numerical scale. This is usually done if the quantitative or integrated method is used. What does this scale mean?

In an *extremely high risk country*, most if not all political risk factors have been asserted in a negative way. On rare occasions it can, however, be only one factor. Expropriations and nationalisations have taken place at a disadvantageous rate for foreign nationals. Under such circumstances, repatriation of capital is nearly impossible, and dividends, interest, fees or royalties are severely controlled and restricted. Payments of trade transactions are in doubt. Business with those countries is usually done only on a government-to-government basis, be it direct or through the addition of a government guarantee for the transaction of a non-governmental institution. Private companies are either locked in due to earlier deals or abstain whenever possible from doing business with such countries. However, if business is successfully done it can be highly profitable – but extremely risky until its completion. Countries in that high class of risk are fairly easily identified. It is, however, much more difficult to see in good time their move in that direction, as well as to perceive their gradual improvement towards a less risky status.

The *very low risk country* on the other end of the scale gives no headaches whatsoever to the foreign investor or lender. It is, however, also the country with the highest competitive environment, as foreigners are keen to invest or lend.

The art of assessing political risk is, therefore, to foresee changes in the risk status of a country in order to optimise potential opportunities and minimise the evolving risks for these purposes. The different risk factors are weighted in relation to each other. The weighting cannot be done uniformly but must be tailor-made for each institution, in order to take into account its special interests. Lenders and investors have different viewpoints. Lenders, for example, usually prefer a strong government with good chances of a long stay in power, regardless of form or political orientation. In addition an institution from a superpower has to use a different approach to assess political risk from one belonging to the group of small neutral countries, because it is *nolens volens* associated with its country of origin.

In order to facilitate the assessment of political risk it might be helpful to apply the same weighting to all countries. This uniformity has, however, serious drawbacks, because it tends to rate the lower risks too well and punish the higher ones too heavily. For a more sophisticated assessment of political risk by means of the quantitative method there should be similar weighting for similar countries only. This could then lead to an early warning system that more quickly identifies risks as well as opportunities. Use of the qualitative methods seems to make it easier to take into account the subtleties of assessing political risk factors, but there is also the drawback of personal prejudice. The quality of the assessors must, therefore, meet a much higher standard for the qualitative system than for the quantitative system.

Qualitative methods

In a purely qualitative approach it is necessary that the evaluation should be based on the teamwork of at least three persons. One member of the team should be a person having a good knowledge of the country in question. This person should have access to first-hand intelligence of the country to be reviewed. This team member should have several years of experience of the country. Another team member should be a political analyst, well trained in the political sciences. His main task would be to cross-check the assumptions made by the country expert in evaluating the different political risk factors. A senior executive with international experience could be the third member of the team. He would lead the team and be responsible for translating its findings into an appropriate strategy for the company. The team would take into account the different political risk factors enumerated and would reach a conclusion on the level of political risk in that country. Such a team could obviously be differently composed according to the type of country and its geographical situation, since nobody is expert in every subject. The team would bring to bear mostly in-house expertise with the exception of the political analyst, who could be recruited from the outside. The problem with this assessment method is that the basis of assessment changes with the different personalities involved.

Another qualitative method is the use of a political adviser who is an expert on the political development of a specific area or country. This approach, also called 'old hands', depends unilaterally on the quality of the expert, and as is known even experts make mistakes. Such experts are usually seasoned diplomats, educators, journalists or businessmen. Their assignments should include assessment of the major political risk factors but are often limited to an assessment of the current leadership and an evaluation of the strengths and weaknesses of the different political groups in a country. Such advisers might be useful for additional insight into a specific area or country from the political point of view, but should not be the deciding factor in evaluating political risk for a major internationally operating institution.

A further qualitative technique is the Delphi method, where the advice of experts is sought in a systematic way. The institution enumerates the different political factors that influence the political future of a nation and then asks a wide group of experts, directly but independently, to rank and weigh the importance of these factors. The results are then assembled in a ranking or index of political risk. The quality of such a ranking – and also its strength or weakness – obviously depends on the choice of factors. It is a fairly unidimensional procedure.

Quantitative method

The quantitative method relies on use of the multivariate analysis, which makes multidimensional decisions possible. The distinguishing feature is that one or several variables are to be the function of other variables. The variables that influence each of the political risk factors must be determined. One can, for example, take the political factor 'constitutional environment'. The variables that make this factor a political risk are the quality of political rights as well as the quality of civil rights. Each of these variables can then be measured on a scale. Added together they can form one of the indicators we are looking for. To make it even more meaningful we can look at this indicator in a dynamic way by screening the development of the two variables over a certain period of time. Thus positive development may be measured on a scale from zero to six and negative development from zero to minus six, as indicated in Tables 5.1 and 5.2.

The formula could then read as follows:

$$\frac{\text{Political rights}}{1983\text{–}87} + \frac{\text{Civil rights}}{1983\text{–}87} = \text{Indicator of changing constitutional environment}$$

Table 5.1. Political rights development, 1983–87

Extraordinary improvement	+6
Substantial improvement	+5
Good improvement	+4
Moderate improvement	+3
Small improvement	+2
Slight improvement	+1
Stable	0
Slight deterioration	−1
Small deterioration	−2
Moderate deterioration	−3
Important deterioration	−4
Substantial deterioration	−5
Extraordinary deterioration	−6

Table 5.2. Civil rights development, 1983–87

Extraordinary improvement	+6
Substantial improvement	+5
Good improvement	+4
Moderate improvement	+3
Small improvement	+2
Slight improvement	+1
Stable	0
Slight deterioration	−1
Small deterioration	−2
Moderate deterioration	−3
Important deterioration	−4
Substantial deterioration	−5
Extraordinary deterioration	−6

The scale of this indicator would then go from minus 12 to plus 12. The difficulty with the method is to find a uniform appraisal of the changes so that a common level for all countries appraised can be found.

Another example might be 'social structure' as a political factor. The political risk of this factor lies in the variables wealth per head, degree of urbanisation, income distribution and degree of literacy. The sensitivity of the political risk is a relation of these variables. The higher the degree of literacy and the higher the wealth per head of population, the lower may be the political risk. The same might also be true for the reverse; i.e. a low literacy and low per capita income usually produce a fairly low political risk. In order to translate this into an indicator we attribute to the degree of literacy the scale one to ten, ten being 100 per cent literacy and one nil. The same goes for GNP per head, which is also measured on a scale of one to ten – assuming ten, for example, for a GNP per head of more than US$10,000. By relating these two variables the sensitivity of the political risk can be measured as shown by the following formula:

$$I_1 = \frac{A}{B}$$

A = Degree of literacy (1–10)
B = GNP per head (1–10)
I_1 = Indicator sensitivity political risk

Graphically, we would have the picture in Fig. 5.1, assuming that there is a linear dependence between the two factors (which is probably not the case).

The formula gives results from one to ten, one being the most stable situation with the lowest probable risk. Another indicator resulting from concern about political risk emanating from the social structure might

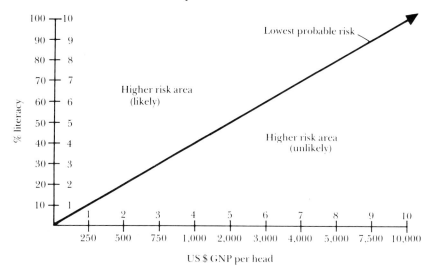

Fig. 5.1. Sensitivity of political risk: two variables

incorporate a third variable such as the distribution of wealth. The difficulty is to relate the three variables, each one being standardised on a one-to-ten scale, in a formula that really indicates the variations in political risk. A multiplication of the indicator 'I_1' by the distribution of wealth variable can give such a result, as in the following formula:

$$I_2 = \frac{A}{B} \times C$$

A = Degree of literacy
B = GNP per head
C = Distribution of wealth
I_2 = Indicator sensitivity political risk

In order to arrive at a good assessment of political risk by using this method, a careful selection of political factors is needed. For each one, the variables must be chosen, quantified and brought into a scaling system.

The variables must then be interrelated in the way that they influence political risk, which can be either through addition, subtraction, multiplication or division. The result of these mathematical calculations gives us one political risk indicator. In order to assess total political risk, the different indicators will then have to be weighted against each other. The difficult tasks in this multivariate system are to find quantifiable variables for each political factor, and the weighting of the different indicators. It is, therefore, advisable to restrict this method to a specific aspect of political risk such as expropriation or nationalisation. The method needs and uses many assumptions and is quite complicated to implement.

The quantitative method can also lead to the scenario approach. It then tries to discover how political risk develops under different assumptions. It is a very interesting approach in so far as it shows that developments are always possible in different directions. The difficulty lies in finding out which are the most probable assumptions.

Integrated method

The third method of assessing political risk is the integrated method, where one tries to bring together the subjective and objective approaches, i.e. the qualitative and quantitative elements. This method benefits from both aspects and is to be recommended for political risk analysis. One would establish a check-list of the political risk factors that are relevant for the type of operation of the institution in question. To each factor variables must be attributed, which then are weighted. For example, one could take the political risk factor 'foreign policy' and evaluate it as follows:

– The foreign policy of the country evaluated in relation to its neighbours, to its belonging to a bloc, to its cultural heritage, is in view of the political risk involved:

	Points
– very comforting	0
– stabilising	2
– no influence	5
– dangerous	8
– very risky	10

This factor would then be weighted in the context of all the other political factors evaluated. The total would come to a certain score, which would then be indexed according to riskiness.

When assessing political risk, it is important that each system also takes into account the time element, because risk has always to be seen in relation to time. Political risk assessment has to deal with a certain time horizon in order to be pertinent. It cannot limit itself to the assessment of the current situation, i.e. the status quo, but must make assumptions about the future and/or find a specific trend. Therefore, the factors that are suitable for it should always take into account a time period of more than one year in order to obtain the needed dynamic approach to the assessment of political risk. It should, however, not lead to pure guesswork.

The intensity of the need for political risk assessment depends on the ultimate aim. It certainly increases in cross-border lending with the lengthening of maturities. In cross-border investments, the need for political risk assessment definitely increases if the size of fixed assets becomes more and more substantial.

Even disregarding the aim of political risk assessment, it must be done systematically for each country with which an institution is involved. This can be every year or every six months, but should certainly take place after an important political event. One cannot assume that the system will become an early warning system after having been in operation within an institution for only six months. Each institution must also discover, by trial and error, the relevant political factors for its own operations. The test period might take several years. It will, however, improve awareness within the institution of political risk, and as time passes, develop more and more into an early warning system regarding that aspect of country risk assessment.

Political risk assessment is one major factor in evaluating the country risk involved in cross-border transactions, the other being transfer risk assessment. Its overall importance will have to be weighed in relation to the importance of this second factor.

6

The economic element: the capability to honour obligations and to incur foreign debt

The economic element – the capability to honour one's obligations and to incur foreign debt – is the other factor to be assessed when evaluating country risk. It is called transfer risk assessment. Transfer risk is easier to quantify than political risk. The current total risk involved is the total of the cross-border liabilities of a country and its institutions. These cross-border liabilities, be they private or public, are usually denominated in the most actively traded international currencies – such as the US dollar, the Deutschmark, the Japanese yen or the Swiss franc. The capability of the country to honour its debt is, therefore, in direct relation to its capability to earn or obtain the necessary foreign exchange in the currency of the debt incurred. Moreover, the country must provide foreign exchange not only for the servicing of its debts as sovereign borrower, but also for the servicing of the cross-border liabilities of private institutions operating within its frontiers.

Transfer risk is, therefore, structured around the relation between a country's current cross-border liabilities as well as its need to incur new debt, and its ability or inability to earn or obtain the necessary foreign exchange to service those liabilities as well as to get new credits. This ability has its origin in the current account balance and the balance of capital movements.

Just as a commercial credit must be paid off through future cash flow or new capital, the cross-border liabilities of a country must be paid off through future foreign exchange earnings or additional capital import. All

40

those factors that have a potential to earn or obtain foreign exchange for the country, or that are a source for the loss of foreign exchange, have to be searched out. It is very important that the institution does not limit itself in its search to only the potential of earning or losing foreign exchange of the country in question; it must also determine whether there are other possibilities of obtaining foreign exchange – basically, foreign credit.

A country will, therefore, have to be examined in view of its economic situation, its production potential, its foreign trade, its inflation and its resources, in order to establish its capability to honour its debts. Furthermore, some countries have, as an additional source of income, construction work abroad and the remittances of persons working abroad. On logical grounds one could assume that the obtaining or earning of foreign exchange by a country is in direct relation to its potential for earning foreign exchange. This is in general correct; however, we have also seen that countries obtain foreign exchange in the financial markets without having the potential to earn it back in the future. Some West European countries, and probably also New Zealand, are examples of such illogical behaviour by the financial markets.

In a first step, a country's foreign exchange operations will be analysed. Foreign exchange is earned or spent only in transactions denominated in foreign currencies, and foreign exchange assets and liabilities are built up only through transactions in such currencies. All economic and political events that influence the foreign exchange operations of a country have, therefore, a bearing on a country's capability to honour its debt. Such events influence the transfer risk of the country involved and, as a result, the country risk itself.

The earning and spending of foreign exchange is in direct relation to a country's international trade activities, namely imports and exports, as well as to its international service activities, i.e. tourism, financial activities, royalty income from licensing agreements, insurance and so on. The building up of foreign exchange assets or incurring of liabilities is a direct result of the difference between the earning and spending of foreign exchange, as well as of transfers for investment – or unilateral transfers such as remittances from nationals working abroad or foreign aid.

Factors influencing foreign exchange operations

Factors within a country's own control

These factors can increase either the inflow or outflow of foreign exchange. They have, depending on their character, an influence on either the current account or capital movements – or on both.

Inflation

Inflation has a significant influence on the foreign exchange operations of a country. We are referring here to home-based inflation. Such inflation has its origin in the economic policy of the country, the main cause normally being an excessively expansionary budget and monetary policy. Inflation as related to inflationary development in the major markets with which the country in question maintains trade relations is the most relevant aspect. Such inflation can be adjusted by the floating of the exchange rate, with only the remaining inflation difference being of relevance. An above-average inflation differential hampers the international competitiveness of an exporter since it means higher labour costs and higher costs for nationally bought semi-products. It usually brings, therefore, a decline in earnings from exports. As such inflation reduces the price of imports, an increase in imports often accompanies the decrease in exports and thus cumulates the negative aspects for the foreign exchange operations of a country. Below-average inflation, on the other hand, benefits foreign exchange operations because it enhances exports and reduces imports. Countries such as West Germany, Japan and Switzerland had the benefits of low inflation rates for many years because of their respective economic policies.

Currency parity policy

The external parity of a country's currency has a major influence on its foreign exchange operations. Currency parity changes were originally used to overcome discrepancies in inflation rates. If a country decides to float its exchange rate, the relation of its currency to all others is formed by the forces of the foreign exchange markets. For the markets it is no longer only inflation discrepancies that change parities. Forecasts, market technicalities, interest developments and political events have become major market movers. Non-floating currencies are still adjusted from time to time to take into account differences in the inflationary development of the major trading partners of the country making the adjustment. The several realignments of the European Monetary System had their cause in such developments.

Devaluation and revaluation are the typical actions undertaken by governments to influence their foreign exchange operations. Through devaluation a government can compensate for the disadvantage in international competitiveness of its exporters due to home-grown inflation, or even try through a competitive devaluation to obtain an advantage for its exporters. The latter action is usually not well received by the international community since it often leads to devaluations by other countries. A devaluation should bring higher exports and reduce imports, thus having a positive cumulative effect on the foreign exchange operations related to

42

trade for the country involved. A substantial drawback does exist, however, since foreign debt and foreign debt service translated into the national currency increase by the percentage of the devaluation. This means that a higher export volume is needed to service the debt.

A less common phenomenon in the currency parity policy of a country is a revaluation of its currency. A revaluation is usually effected to cool down the domestic economy. It increases imports and reduces inflation and debt service on the foreign debt. The revaluation can also occur if a country does not want to adapt its exchange rate to a realistic level despite the fact that the economic situation would make it necessary. Such a silent revaluation can lead to unwanted capital outflow or even capital flight, as was the case in Mexico and Venezuela in the early 1980s.

Within this complex of currency parity policy also fall all the regulations that ministries of finance and central banks issue to control the flow of money across national borders. There are broadly four types of regimes with variations. The two extremes are either no foreign exchange control or full foreign exchange control. Between these two extremes we find control of capital movements, or control of capital movements as well as of trade and services, in different shades.

Table 6.1 provides a survey of exchange rates and arrangements at end-September 1984.

Economic policies

Economic policies have a major bearing on the external accounts of a country. They fix the way in which a national economy is managed. They influence the division of the economy into state and private sectors. They create or eliminate the incentives for efficiency in all sectors of the economy. They are responsible for the state of public finances and influence inflation. Sound economic policies create a favourable climate not only for investments in the country, but also for an efficient production structure that can be competitive in international markets. Looking at economic policies, it is also worth while determining the position of the central bank within the policy-making process of a country. An independent central bank normally allows at least some economic policies to be executed by an independent body. In addition, the use of the printing press to solve budgetary problems is discounted.

Use of foreign funds

A factor often neglected in the past is the actual use that is made of funds that a country borrows abroad. This is, obviously, especially true of sovereign borrowing; the utilisation of borrowed funds by private entities is normally project-orientated and, therefore, easily recognised. Sovereign borrowing is also used for project financing that helps develop the country

43

Table 6.1 Exchange rates and exchange arrangements, 31 December 1986

Member (currency)	Exchange rate pegged to	Exchange rate[1]	Exchange rate otherwise determined[2,3]
Afghanistan (Afghani)[4]			50.60
Algeria (dinar)[4]	bskt	4.8235	
Antigua and Barbuda (EC$)[5]	$	2.70	
Argentina (austral) (12/30)			1.2570
Australia (dollar)			1.50421
Austria (schilling)	bskt	13.71	
Bahamas, The (dollar)[4]	$	1.00	
Bahrain (dinar)[6]			0.376
Bangladesh (taka)[4]	bskt	30.80	
Barbados (dollar)	$	2.0113	
Belgium (franc)[4,7]			40.41
Belize (dollar)	$	2.00	
Benin (franc)	F	50.00	
Bhutan (ngultrum)	Re	1.00	
Bolivia (peso)			1,923,000.0
Botswana (pula)	bskt	1.83756	
Brazil (cruzado)[8,9]			14.865
Burkina Faso (franc)	F	50.00	
Burma (kyat)	SDR	8.5085	6.956
Burundi (franc)	SDR	151.5	123.856
Cameroon (franc)	F	50.00	
Canada (dollar)			1.3805
Cape Verde (escudo)	bskt	76.5697	
Central African Republic (franc)	F	50.00	
Chad (franc)	F	50.00	
Chile (peso)[4,8,9]			195.04
China (renminbi)			3.7221
Colombia (peso)[8]			205.56
Comoros (franc)	F	50.00	
Congo (franc)	F	50.00	
Costa Rica (colón)[4]			53.70
Cyprus (pound)	bskt	0.511640	
Denmark (krone)[7]			7.3425
Dijbouti (franc)	$	177.721	
Dominica (EC$)[5]	$	2.70	
Dominican Rep. (peso)			3.0766

Member (currency)	Exchange rate pegged to	Exchange rate[1]	Exchange rate otherwise determined
Ecuador (sucre)[10]			
Egypt (pound)	$	0.70	
El Salvador (colón)[10]	$		
Equatorial Guinea (franc)	F	50.00	
Ethiopia (birr)	$	2.07	
Fiji (dollar)	bskt	1.14534	
Finland (markka)[11]	bskt	4.794	
France (franc)[7] (12/30)			6.4
Gabon (franc)	F	50.00	
Gambia, The, (dalasi)			7.4
Germany, Fed. Rep. of, (Deutschmark)[7]			1.9
Ghana (cedi)[4]	$		90.0
Greece (drachma)			138.7
Grenada (EC$)[5]	$	2.70	
Guatemala (quetzal)[4]	$	1.00	
Guinea (franc)	$		400.0
Guinea-Bissau (peso)			238.9
Guyana (dollar)	bskt	4.40	
Haiti (gourde)	$	5.00	
Honduras (lempira)	$	2.00	
Hungary (forint)	bskt	45.9269	
Iceland (króna)			40.2
India (rupee)[12] (12/30)			13.1
Indonesia (rupiah)			1641.0
Iran, Islamic Rep. of, (rial)	SDR	92.30	75.4
Iraq (dinar)	$	0.310857	
Ireland (punt)[7]			0.7
Israel (new shekel)			1.4
Italy (lira)[7] (12/30)			1358.1
Ivory Coast (franc)	F	50.00	
Jamaica (dollar)			5.4
Japan (yen)			160.0
Jordan (dinar)	SDR	0.4098	0.3
Kenya (shilling)[11]	SDR	19.6441	16.0
Kiribati (dollar)	A$	1.003	

Member (currency)	Exchange rate pegged to	Exchange rate[1]	Exchange rate otherwise determined[2,3]
:a (won)			861.40
~ait (dinar)	bskt	0.29276	
People's Dem. ~p. (kip)[4]	$	10.00	
~non (pound)[10]			
~tho (loti)[4]	R	1.00	
~ria (dollar)	$	1.00	
~a (dinar)[13]	SDR	0.383929	0.313875
~mbourg ~anc)[4,7]			40.630
~lagascar (franc)[8]			769.8086
~awi (kwacha)	bskt	1.9524	
~aysia (ringgit)[11]	bskt	2.6015	
~dives (rufiyaa)	bskt	7.2443	
~i (franc)	F	50.00	
~ta (lira)	bskt	0.369140	
~ritania ~uguiya)	bskt	74.08	
~uritius (rupee)	bskt	13.1367	
~ico (peso)[4] (2/30)			923.5
~occo (dirham)			8.7117
~ambique ~etical)[10]	bskt	39.2365	
~al (rupee)	bskt	22.0	
~erlands, The, ~uilder)[7]			2.192
~Zealand ~ollar)			1.90658
~ragua ~órdoba)[4]	$	70.00	
~r (franc)	F	50.00	
~ria (naira)[4]			3.5121
~vay (krone)	bskt	7.40	
~an (rial Omani)	$	0.3845	
~stan (rupee)[10]			
~ama (balboa)	$	1.00	
~ua New Guinea ~ina)	bskt	0.961169	
~guay (guarani)[4]	$	160.00	
~ (inti)[4]	$	13,942.77	
~ppines (peso) (2/29)			20.53
Poland (zloty)	bskt	197.620	
Portugal (escudo)[8]			146.117
Qatar (riyal)[6]			3.64
Romania (leu)[10]	bskt		
Rwanda (franc)	SDR	102.71	83.9690
St. Christopher and Nevis (EC$)[5]	$	2.70	
St. Lucia (EC$)[5]	$	2.70	
St. Vincent (EC$)[5]	$	2.70	
São Tomé and Principe (dobra)	SDR	45.25	36.9934
Saudi Arabia (riyal)[6]			3.745
Senegal (franc)	F	50.00	
Seychelles (rupee)	SDR	7.2345	5.91445
Sieera Leone (leone)			35.7143
Singapore (dollar)	bskt	2.175	
Solomon Islands (dollar)	bskt	1.98649	
Somalia (shilling)[4,8]			90.5
South Africa (rand)[4]			2.18341
Spain (peseta) (12/30)			132.395
Sri Lanka (rupee)			28.52
Sudan (pound)[4]	bskt	2.50	
Suriname (guilder)	$	1.785	
Swaziland (lilangeni)	R	1.00	
Sweden (krona)[14] (12/30)	bskt	6.819	
Syrian Arab Rep. (pound)[4]	$	3.925	
Tanzania (shilling)	bskt	51.7189	
Thailand (baht)	bskt	26.13	
Togo (franc)	F	50.00	
Tonga (pa'anga)	A$	1.00	
Trinidad and Tobago (dollar)	$	3.609	
Tunisia (dinar)			0.843793
Turkey (lira)			757.79
Uganda (shilling)	$	1,400.0	
United Arab Emirates (dirham)[6]			3.671

45

Table 6.1. – cont.

Member (currency)	Exchange rate pegged to	Exchange rate[1]	Exchange rate otherwise deter-mined[2,3]	Member (currency)	Exchange rate pegged to	Exchange rate[1]	Exchange rate otherwise deter-mined
United Kingdom (pound)			0.681663	Yugoslavia (dinar)			457.1
United States (dollar)			1.00	Zaïre (zaïre)			71.1
Uruguay (new peso)			181.0	Zambia (kwacha)			12.7
Vanuatu (vatu)	SDR	142.00		Zimbabwe (dollar)	bskt	1.67813	
Venezuela (bolivar)[4]	$	7.50	116.090				
Vietnam (new dong)[4,10]							
Western Samoa (tala)			2.19780				
Yemen Arab Rep. (rial)	$	7.24					
Yemen, People's Dem. Rep. (dinar)	$	0.345399					

$	US Dollar
F	French franc
R	South African rand
bskt	Currency basket other than SDR
Re	Indian rupee
A$	Australian dollar

1. Rates as reported to the Fund and in terms of currency units per unit listed; rates determined by baskets of currencies are in currency units per US dollar.
2. Market rates in currency units per US dollar.
3. Under this heading are listed those members who describe their exchange rate arrangements as floating independently or as adjusting according to a set of indicators (see footnote 8) and certain other members whose exchange arrangements are not otherwise described in this table. In addition, US dollar quotations are given for the currencies that are pegged to the SDR and for those that participate in the European Monetary System (see footnote 7).
4. Member maintains dual exchange markets involving multiple exchange arrangements. The arrangement shown is that maintained in the major market. A description of the member's exchange system as of December 31 1985 is given in the *Annual Report on Exchange Arrangements and Exchange Restrictions, 1986.*
5. East Caribbean dollar.
6. Exchange rates are determined on the basis of a relationship to the SDR, within margins of ± 7.25 per cent. However, because of the maintenance of a relatively stable relationship with the US dollar, these margins are not always observed.

7. Belgium, Denmark, France, the Federal Republic Germany, Ireland, Italy, Luxembourg, and The Netherlands are participating in the exchange rate and intervention mechanism of the European Monetary System maintain maximum margins of 2.25 per cent (in the of the Italian lira, 6 per cent) for exchange rate transactions in the official markets between their currencies and those of the other countries in this group.
8. Exchange rates adjusted to a set of indicators.
9. Member maintains a system of advance announcement of exchange rates.
10. Exchange rate data not available.
11. The exchange rate is maintained within margins of ± per cent.
12. The exchange rate is maintained within margins of per cent on either side of a weighted composite of currencies of the main trading partners.
13. The exchange rate is maintained within margins of ± per cent.
14. The exchange rate is maintained within margins of ± per cent.

Data: IMF Treasurer's and Exchange and Trade Relations Departments

Source: International Monetary Fund survey, 23 February 1987.

as well as its economy. And it can be used to develop industries that have an import substitution effect by creating domestic production as a replacement for imported goods. Another use can be the financing of a balance-of-payments deficit that has its origin in a deficit of the balance of trade or of the current account. Funds can, however, also be borrowed to finance a budget deficit of the central or local governments, which can have its origin in many different reasons that are more or less acceptable. Deficit spending to maintain a welfare state or to keep up subsidies for food or desolate industries has certainly less appeal to foreign lenders than the building of a sensible infrastructure for a growing economy.

The use of these funds can, therefore, create a new potential for foreign exchange earnings, or have a directly opposite effect by expanding the need for foreign exchange through increased foreign debt. A careful analysis should thus be made on the use of funds in order to find out where borrowed funds are going. This is not always an easy undertaking. Studying the budgets as well as the accounts of the central government of the country one is evaluating is helpful in this context. Through a responsible policy of usage of funds, the borrowing country can influence its standing with foreign lenders and, consequently, its ability to obtain foreign exchange.

Terms of trade and services

The development of the terms of trade and services, i.e. a country's position as a contributor and user of cross-border trade and services, has a significant influence on the country's foreign exchange operations. Inflation and currency parity policy are not the only influences on the terms of trade and services. The relation between self-sufficiency and domestic demand, for example, can develop in a negative way because of structural changes in production and demand, thereby affecting the terms of trade and services. These structural changes occurred in the 1960s and early 1970s at a relatively slow pace and, therefore, did not abruptly disturb the foreign exchange operations of a country. Some more recent examples, such as the car and steel industries, the revolution in electronic consumer goods, the development of new watches and the much higher return on food production per acre in Europe have had, however, a rather fast impact on the terms of trade of the countries concerned. Terms of trade are also influenced by the ingenuity, adaptability and dynamism of a country's population.

Natural resources

Natural resources are a major factor in a country's potential for economic development. They can help reduce imports or be the source of substantial export earnings. The most pertinent point is the way in which the country's authorities deplete these natural resources. The stretching out currently practised by Norway for its oil resources is one policy, whereas cash-strapped, high-absorbing oil-exporting countries run their output at a very high level.

47

Customs levies and excise taxes

The use of customs levies was, until the early 1960s, not only a means of protecting domestic industry, but also a tool for managing the foreign exchange operations of a country as well as a substantial source of income for many countries' budgets. Through the work of GATT, customs levies have lost their significance in many parts of the world and for many products, especially manufactured goods. They are, however, still applied to restrict the import of certain goods, often called luxury goods, to protect the foreign exchange situation of a specific country. Import deposits have a similar aim. In addition, many non-tariff barriers have been created to protect home industries, which indirectly helps save foreign exchange.

Management of foreign debt

It would seem obvious that management of foreign debt would be of prime importance to a country with a foreign debt. It is, therefore, quite astonishing to see the differences in the quality of foreign debt management by heavily indebted nations around the world. The World Bank is playing a major role in helping countries to improve the collection and processing of debt information. Especially in the fields of unguaranteed and short-term debt, much still remains to be done to improve knowledge about one's own situation. A well-structured debt that is limited only by the market acceptability of a country can optimise the use of foreign exchange. The management of debt should also include the management of a country's reserve position.

Capital movements and unilateral transfers

Capital movements can have a very detrimental but also beneficial effect on the foreign exchange operations of a country. Under their most negative aspect capital movements become capital flight. They are then a source of loss of foreign exchange that should not be underestimated. Capital flight takes place primarily because the economic and political climate does not provide the necessary incentive for accumulating capital in one's own country. It is, therefore, definitely a factor that is under a country's own control. The inflow of foreign capital for investment helps not only to broaden the economic base but also brings foreign exchange with it. Many countries have seen the beneficial aspects of this and have, therefore, created special development agencies, such as the Irish Development Agency. In a more specialised form, such capital is provided under the terms of foreign aid. Remittances of savings by people working abroad must also be included here. They fluctuate substantially according to the trust placed by the workers in their own country, which was, for example, manifest after the revolution in Portugal in 1974. They are an important source of foreign exchange for many countries that have people working abroad.

Trade barriers

Trade barriers, either quantitative or qualitative, are a typical case where a country's ability to earn foreign exchange can be seriously impaired. While the free flow of goods and the fight against protectionism find many supporters in influential circles world-wide, the actual situation is quite different. Trade wars are going on between the major blocs and nations. Agricultural policies are mostly excluded from the fight against protectionism and, therefore, this important segment of international trade has not received the free trade label. Trade barriers normally have a negative effect on the foreign exchange operations of all countries concerned. They often support dying industries in industrialised countries, with an ever-increasing cost to the community. Developing countries use trade barriers to protect their new industries, which can be at the cost of efficiency.

Commodity prices

The development of commodity prices is usually beyond the influence of a specific country. Price fluctuations, however, very much affect the foreign exchange operations of the countries that are the main producers of commodities. In order to eliminate excessively wide fluctuations, buffer stocks and cartels have been proposed. But these ideas, which can certainly help the producer, are fairly difficult to implement. For example, many agricultural products can be stored for only a limited period of time. Furthermore, stocks have to be very substantial in order to be used as buffer stocks. This causes problems not only for storage of these stocks but also for financing them. Who should really finance them – the producer or the consumer? The International Monetary Fund has created a special facility for countries that have been adversely affected by movements in commodity prices. Only in the case of oil has a cartel worked in favour of the producers for several years, i.e. OPEC. It has certainly had beneficial effects for some countries, but raised unfulfillable expectations in others and created grave economic problems in many. In addition, this cartel was one of the major causes of the disruption of the world economy in the late 1970s. In the mid-1980s it started to disintegrate.

Interest rates

Because foreign debt or trade credit is incurred in foreign currencies, the interest rate on those liabilities is fixed by the international financial markets – which is beyond the influence of most countries. The rate of interest has, however, a very direct effect on the foreign exchange operations of the countries involved. The higher the rate, the more foreign exchange is needed. The widespread use of the floating interest rate as the price for international credit has added another element of uncertainty to the management of the foreign debt of a country, because the amounts needed change constantly. Preferential rates are applied by the International Development Agency (IDA), as well as in foreign aid.

Natural catastrophes

Natural catastrophes have a bearing mainly on smaller and less-developed countries. They mostly affect the agricultural sector with the destruction of harvests. This leads to additional imports and, therefore, to a loss of foreign exchange. While natural catastrophes are quite unpredictable, their effects are often reduced through international aid programmes. It is, however, possible that the destruction of the ecological balance occurring in many countries will lead to unmanageable problems for them in the future. One might, therefore, see new risks in this direction that are for the time being difficult to evaluate.

Transportation

Cross-border transactions of goods and services usually also involve transportation. While the costs of transportation are often not within the control of the country, they can have an important impact on its exports or imports. They can price a country out of a market. Not only can the costs of transportation be a problem but also its availability, as was shown by the closing of the Suez Canal in 1967.

Market conditions

Market conditions are a factor outside the control of most countries. They are an important factor in several respects. Market conditions are principally influenced by market liquidity. As we talk about the global financial market we have to take into account all the major money and capital markets. They tend to depend on each other and balance each other out, as long as monetary policies in the major countries do not hinder this. Of all the markets, the situation on the Euromarket is of prime importance since it is the major provider of funds for cross-border lending. Abundant liquidity usually leads to easier borrowing and lending, as all banks tend to be builders of assets in such times. This was, as is known, one of the reasons leading to the substantial buildup of debt by the developing countries at the end of the 1970s. But not only is liquidity an important factor, allocating funds and deciding on the maturities available for lending; the emotional state of the market is important as well. If everybody wants to stay short because an increase in interest rates is expected, it will be difficult to obtain long-term funds. The shortening of final maturities from 12 years to seven over a period of two years between 1979 and 1981 was also more an emotional than a rational exercise, especially since floating rates were the norm for those kinds of credit, and the forecasting of a country's performance over a period of seven as well as 12 years has a similar degree of uncertainty. As every banker knows, allocation of funds or acquisition of assets is achieved by taking into account the expected return as well as the potential risk. While decisions are always supposed to be made by looking at the optimum between risk and return, the concept of the optimum is fairly strongly influenced by expectations such as those of the market. As we have seen by looking at the participants in the different rescheduling exercises, only very few bankers are strong enough to go against a specific trend or expectation, even if it sometimes runs against the basics of an optimum relation between risk and return. While these bankers may at the time of their decision look like black sheep, they have to be qualified as the really smart bankers at the end of the day.

Concessional funds

These can be obtained only by the developing countries. They are concessional because they bear an interest rate below the market rate and/or have a maturity that is much longer than what is available in international markets. Major suppliers of concessional funds are governments and supranational bodies. Concessional funds are, therefore, either negotiated bilaterally between governments or are available after a credit and project assessment by one of the supranational bodies such as the IDA. The availability of these funds does not follow market patterns but rather political developments in the industrialised world. In the 1960s and 1970s, electorates in most industrialised countries were convinced that concessional funds had to be made available for the developing world. Today the situation has changed under the constraints of national budgets. The 1 per cent of GNP for foreign aid as a guideline for the OECD countries is no longer as widely accepted as before, even in a country like Sweden. As mentioned, the possibility of obtaining concessional funds is limited to the developing countries. The poorer the country is, the more important is this source of funds.

Factors influencing the capability to obtain foreign credits

It seems that there are also factors that give a country the capability to incur foreign debts by disregarding the primary reasons for it, i.e. the potential of earning foreign exchange.

Size of the economy

The size of a country's economy influences its ability to obtain foreign credits. The larger the economy of a country, the more capability it has to obtain foreign credits – according to an opinion that size is an insurance against the perils of foreign exchange operations. Therefore, a GNP above US$300 billion would make a country a better transfer risk than would a GNP below US$100 million. This assumption needs to be proved.

GNP per head

High GNP per head means that the country is considered rich. Such countries seem to have easier access to cross-border funds than do poor countries. This fact is not based on an analytical appreciation and neglects the observation that transfer risk is basically a risk of debt service and not of substance.

Belonging to an economic grouping

Countries that belong to an economic group such as the EEC or Comecon have often benefited or suffered because of this, irrespective of their individual standing. The famous umbrella theory was buried only when it was crystal clear that the USSR would not support Poland and Romania economically. The difficulties for all Comecon countries in obtaining cross-border credit after the Polish and Romanian crises were the reverse effect.

These three factors probably have their origin in the credit appraisal system for commercial credits. Credit officers often look first for security and can, therefore, succumb to the thinking that a large company is a better credit risk than a smaller one, that a rich man is a better risk than a poor one, or that having an important relation or belonging to an impressive conglomerate is a better risk than to be on one's own. History has, however, shown that these are dangerous assumptions. The same holds true for the assessment of transfer risk. While these factors influence the capability of a country to obtain foreign credits, they are of minor importance if we look at a country's capability to earn foreign exchange.

The external debt

We tried earlier to analyse the different factors that influence the foreign exchange earning potential of a country. As we would like to measure that potential through the indicators, it is obviously also necessary to evaluate the yardstick against which we are to measure. These are the cross-border liabilities of a country or, in short, its external debt. In order to obtain a meaningful figure we must know the structure of this debt. Its four major elements are the total amount, the maturity profile, the currencies involved and the interest rates.

The total amount of the external debt should include public-sector debt, publicly guaranteed debt and private debt. The maturity profile, i.e. the schedule of repayments for all three parts of the external debt, should be known. The maturity profile should be structured in such a way that it is clearly evident when each part is coming due. Short-term debt up to one year should be identified, as well as longer-term debt, usually structured according to the year when it comes due. The maturity profile should, therefore, incorporate the repayment schedule of each cross-border liability. A breakdown along currency lines is interesting because of its relation to the country's export profile. It can indicate potential foreign currency risks or a substantial matching of foreign currency debt and export income. It is especially interesting for countries that have an external debt in convertible and non-convertible currencies. Through the interest rates we obtain the yearly payments for interest. This figure can, however, only be an estimate if debt with floating interest rates is involved, as these rates change at regular intervals over the lifetime of the debt. Interest payments for one year added to the repayments due in that specific year gives us the so-called debt service for that year.

In addition to this breakdown, it is of interest to distinguish the different creditors of a country. We usually find four major categories: governments and their different export credit agencies, supranational institutions such as the International Monetary Fund and World Bank, the international banking community, and investors, namely individuals and corporations.

It might be thought that it is fairly easy to obtain the necessary figures for the total external debt of a country and for its structure. This is, unfortunately, not so; no country or institution publishes the external debt according to the standards outlined above. In all the reschedulings that have been carried out so far, it was always an extremely onerous task to try to find out the exact amounts of outstanding debt. While data were usually available for certain parts of the external debt, they were not at all for other parts. Even countries with state-controlled economies were not in a much better position.

As countries normally have not only external debts but also external assets, such as the reserve position of the central bank, these assets must be assessed as well. The reserve position is of particular importance since it gives an indication of the international liquidity of a country. Part of the reserves are sometimes held in gold. It is, therefore, important to value that part at the correct market rate. Furthermore, the reserves or part of them are sometimes pledged against short-term or bridge financing by supranational institutions. To ascertain the pledged amount of the reserves is usually very difficult unless it is public knowledge. In addition to the reserve position, banks, corporations and individuals often hold foreign assets. Foreign banking assets, especially if they are of a short-term nature, are better netted with the liabilities instead of taking them separately into account. The foreign assets of corporations and individuals can be of significance only if they are matched by liabilities of the same corporations and individuals. In this case they can be offset against each other. For all other cases it is better not to take them into account since it will be fairly difficult to mobilise these assets to meet a country's obligations. In addition, very often the foreign assets of individuals are black money and, therefore, even more difficult to trace. Only confidence in one's own country will mobilise those reserves as was shown by a return flow of private money into Mexico after the declaration of austerity measures by the government of President de la Madrid.

In connection with the establishment of the external debt of a specific country, it is also important to know if there exist any open credits not yet used. Every member country of the International Monetary Fund has, for example, several regular quotas on which it can draw. These quotas enable them to take care of short-term balance-of-payments difficulties. They have been increased regularly with the general adjustment of the quotas. The Bank for International Settlements publishes figures for open credits supplied by the private banking systems of the 14 reporting countries on a regular basis. Open credit lines enable a country to manage its short-term liquidity position on the one hand, but usually lead on the other hand to an increased total external debt at a later stage. It is important to take open credit lines into account to obtain as complete a picture as possible.

The last point to be raised under the heading of external debt is the cross-border liabilities that are only potential ones. This kind of liability arises, for instance, from the planned return on a foreign investment. As long as the market is growing and the confidence of investors is maintained, the return on the investment is often not transferred but reinvested. This changes, however, as soon as the investor feels that the risk is increasing. He will use all available means, such as artificial transfer prices, special head office charges, overvaluation of imports, undervaluation of exports and so on. As many countries have very strict control over foreign investments, they will argue that they can always influence this potential source of loss of foreign exchange through specific legislation. This is certainly true, but one should not underestimate the attraction of foreign investments due to a fairly liberal attitude towards remittance of profits. In many cases, however, this aspect of external debt can be neglected, since its size is difficult to estimate and is usually of minor importance in relation to the total external debt.

Indicators to measure transfer risk

Having analysed the factors that influence the foreign exchange operations and foreign debt situation of a country, with some observations on external debt, we should now try to find the indicators that measure transfer risk. Transfer risk increases if the availability of foreign exchange and foreign borrowing for a country is deteriorating and improves if availability is increasing. A change in the quality of transfer risk can be due to short-term changes in one or several of the factors enumerated. In this case we should talk of a liquidity problem. However, a change can also be the result of circumstances that have evolved over many years, so that solvency has been changing. We will revert to this differentiation when we assess transfer risk. Of the many indicators available and used, those which are best known and most pertinent will be described.

Debt service ratio

This indicator measures the payments for servicing the external debt over a certain period of time in relation to total foreign exchange income during the same period of time. The payment for servicing the external debt consists of interest payments as well as the principal due measured for debt with maturity over one year. Foreign exchange income is computed in its totality and comprises income from exports and services as well as income from unilateral transfers. The debt service ratio is usually measured for a period of one year, with development over the years being compared. It is expressed in a percentage figure:

$$\text{Debt service ratio} = \frac{\text{interest and principal on external debt with maturity over one year over period } N}{\text{foreign exchange income over period } N}$$

Debt service ratio is also forecast for future periods. While the necessary payments of the external debt can be compiled, the income side is subject to many assumptions and is, therefore, difficult to forecast. The lower the ratio, the better. A debt service ratio of 10 per cent and less is considered very good. Above 25 per cent is already viewed as a fairly difficult situation in the context of transfer risk.

As debt service ratio is a relation between two figures, its development depends on the development of each of the two figures. The greater volatility is found in the development of principal and foreign exchange income. Interest payments, on the other hand, are more stable. An improvement in the debt service ratio can, therefore, have its origin in a substantially reduced principal because of the maturity profile or in a changing foreign exchange income.

Debt service ratios for public and publicly guaranteed debt of certain major developing countries between 1970 and 1985 were as follows:

	1970	1975	1980	1985
Brazil	12.5	17.9	34.5	26.6
Mexico	23.6	24.9	32.1	36.9
South Korea	19.5	11.6	12.3	15.2
India	23.7	13.3	8.4	13.3
Algeria	3.9	9.4	26.6	33.3

Source: World Bank, *World Debt Tables 1986/87*.

The major drawback of the debt service ratio is that it assumes that the country in question can repay its debts out of its own resources. This is normally not possible since a continuous import of capital goods is necessary to maintain current export performance, the more so if it should be increased. This is also why a 10 per cent debt service ratio is considered good, because such a ratio leaves ample room for needed expenditure on imports. It would be fairly unwise to assume that the transfer risk is only minimal because of a 10 per cent debt service ratio, as the debt service ratio gives no indication if a country runs a positive current account or not and must, therefore, be considered to be a ratio that measures solvency more than liquidity. A better ratio would be one that measures the result of the current account balance against the amounts needed for interest and principal payments. This would clearly show the difficult situation of many countries in managing their external debt, as the ratios would often be negative. Even if we take only the necessary payments for interest into account the situation is still alarming, since every country with an external debt but not a positive current account balance cannot match its interest payments. With the exception of the oil-exporting countries, however, a better situation is difficult to achieve for most of the developing countries.

The debt service ratio is, nevertheless, a very well known and widely accepted ratio. Especially in comparing it over a certain period of years, it gives an indication of the development of a country's transfer risk. But it must also be borne in mind that short-term external debt is always excluded. As noted above, it would be fairly unwise to assume that transfer risk is minimal with a ten per cent ratio and, therefore, a direct translation of debt service ratio into a specific transfer risk should not be made. Such reasoning has often led to superficial assessment of transfer risks in the past.

A variation of the debt service ratio is the current investment ratio, which differs from the former in that it includes profits and dividends from private foreign investments in addition to the foreign exchange earnings of a country. It therefore adds incoming and outgoing foreign exchange to the denominator. The inclusion of the return on investment is certainly of importance in countries that have substantial foreign investments in relation to their total production basis. It has been said that its inclusion is superfluous since it is in direct relation to export earnings and, therefore, taken into account through the development of foreign exchange earnings from exports. For investments in export industries this might be true, but more and more developing countries are also interested in import substitution industries. Returns on such investments, however, do not follow the pattern of exports. It is thus advisable to take the return on foreign investments, be it dividends or other sorts of remuneration, into account when measuring the overall external claims against a country. In practice, it will again be very difficult to obtain such a figure because investment service payments are never computed.

As has been noted, the debt service ratio has several drawbacks. There have been different suggestions to overcome them. One is to average out interest payments and principal due by adding that charge over several years and then dividing the total by the number of years used. Such a method focuses more on the solvency aspect of a country, therefore neglecting the liquidity problems that can suddenly erupt due to a high debt service obligation in one year. The same can also be applied to the denominator which measures exports where a prognosis has to be made. The averaging out of projected exports should probably be done over a fairly short period, e.g. three years, in order to give a useful indication.

Another drawback of the debt service ratio is that it neglects the extent to which imports have been or can be compressed to compensate for foreign exchange shortage. While this is obviously true, it is very difficult to assess the extent to which such a development is possible. Furthermore, the traditional debt service ratio omits the income from currency reserves as well as foreign investments. This income is, however, only of minor importance for many LDCs.

While the debt service ratio is no perfect indicator to measure a country's ability to service its external debt, it is, nevertheless, the most widely used one. We thus find it in the *World Debt Tables* of the World Bank as one of the major indicators. It would appear to be a useful indicator that can be helpful in assessing transfer risk. It should always be used in its original form in order not to lead to confusion when debt service ratios of several countries are compared.

Debt/GNP ratio

This is a ratio which assumes that the relation between total external debt and gross national product has an influence on transfer risk. It normally excludes short-term debt up to one year. The ratio is measured in a percentage figure:

$$\text{Debt/GNP ratio} = \frac{\text{external public and private debt}}{\text{GNP}}$$

The higher the ratio, the higher the risk involved. A ratio below 15 per cent is considered very acceptable, while a ratio over 30 per cent is already viewed as a very difficult situation. This statement, however, must be qualified. First of all, the components of GNP must be known and analysed. A highly export-orientated country has a different potential to incur external debt than a country that creates its GNP internally, because such an economy earns relatively more foreign exchange to service its level of debt than the other. A substantial public sector offers better control over inflow and outflow of foreign exchange, but hampers the flexibility of a country's economy and, therefore, its ability to adjust to a changing situation. On the other hand, the size of the GNP involved can also be of importance, because a large GNP tends to appeal more to lenders than a smaller one. The debt/GNP ratio is one that looks more at the solvency of a country than at its liquidity. It cannot be used as an early warning indicator to spot liquidity problems but is useful in assessing the overall creditworthiness of a country in international financial markets.

Interest service ratio

This is derived from the debt service ratio and corresponds to the following equation:

$$\text{Interest service ratio} = \frac{\text{interest payment over period } N}{\substack{\text{exports of goods and all services} \\ \text{over period } N}}$$

In contrast to the debt service ratio it focuses more on the liquidity aspects of external debt exposure, while still excluding short-term external debt under one year. It is by definition always a lower percentage than the debt service ratio. The difference in per cent between the two ratios shows the percentage of exports of goods and services needed each year to service the principal. It is, therefore, also of interest to look at the difference between the two. Table 6.2 shows a comparison of these differences for Brazil, India and Israel.

An increasing interest service ratio shows that more and more of the exports of goods and services are needed just to service interest payments on the foreign debt. The change in the difference between the two ratios, however, gives some indication about the development of the structure of the external debt. A decreasing difference indicates that the country was in a position to repay part of its external debt or to stretch it and, therefore, to obtain a better maturity profile of its debt. The interest service ratio is, therefore, a good complement to the debt service ratio.

Table 6.2. Comparison of debt/interest service ratios

		1975	1980	1985
		%		
Brazil:	Debt service ratio	17.9	34.5	26.6
	Interest service ratio	8.6	18.0	21.5
	Difference	9.3	16.5	5.1
India:	Debt service ratio	13.3	8.4	13.3
	Interest service ratio	4.4	3.0	5.6
	Difference	8.9	5.4	7.7
Israel:	Debt service ratio	19.3	14.2	19.7
	Interest service ratio	5.7	7.8	12.4
	Difference	13.6	6.4	7.3

Source: World Bank, *World Debt Tables*, 1986/87.

Liquidity ratios

While until the late 1970s concern was mainly with the solvency of a country and, therefore, the inclination was to look only at the medium-term situation, the rescheduling wave that started in late 1981 showed the importance of liquidity for a country's performance in international financial markets. In commercial lending terms, liquidity ratios would be called the acid test or the quick ratio. The difficulty with these ratios is that by the time the different factors have been statistically established, the situation has already changed. The only development that can easily be measured is the late payment experience. This experience has to be judged in order to see if it is only a technical matter or really an indication of a worsening of the situation. Nevertheless, it is certainly worth while looking at some of these liquidity ratios.

Reserves/imports

This ratio relates a country's currency reserves to its imports. It measures the country's ability to pay for its imports with current liquid assets. It is normally expressed in one month's coverage. The reserves of the country are the officially published reserves. If gold is part of the reserves, an adjustment in relation to its market price should be made.

Imports must be estimated by using an average of at least the past six months, unless the country shows extreme seasonal volatility in its imports. As long as the reserves cover more than a five months' average of imports, liquidity can be considered as highly sufficient, whereas a one month's average means a critical situation that needs careful watching. Countries with low coverage of import requirements often have stand-by arrangements with the international financial community that allow them to overcome a sudden liquidity gap. This is especially true of many OECD countries and the more developed Comecon countries, so that they usually have very low import coverage ratios. For these countries, therefore, the ratio loses its significance.

The reserve/import ratio clearly focuses on the short end of the country's external liabilities. However, it omits interest and principal payments needed to service the external debt. This is again a drawback since imports can always be compressed, whereas debt service such as interest payments and principal due is fixed regarding rate, amount and payment day and can be altered only after negotiation. It is also a questionable ratio for smaller countries that have an atypical export/import structure.

Liquidity gap ratio

This ratio is designed to foresee how a country can manage its short-term financial requirements. The liquidity one measures is that needed to cover the liabilities of the coming year. It consists of the one-year short-term debt minus the balance on the current account. Such a calculation gives a gap in liquidity if the total figure is positive. This gap can in normal times be reduced through taking up Eurodeposits and can therefore be adjusted by an estimated figure of obtainable Eurodeposits. The thus estimated liquidity gap is then measured against projected foreign exchange income from exports, services and unilateral transfers for the coming year. Under normal market conditions one can assume that a liquidity gap ratio of 20 per cent can be covered through additional short-term borrowings. The reasoning behind this ratio is that, bearing in mind changing market conditions, it will always be possible to fund a liquidity gap of a certain size as a measure to overcome short-term liquidity problems. The higher the percentage of the liquidity gap ratio, however, the more difficult it will be for the country concerned to manage successfully its short-term financial requirements.

Other indicators relating to the liquidity of a country can be added to the one above. But they are sometimes more difficult to grasp. The development of reserves and especially large losses are certainly signs of change in the liquidity situation of a country. In the case of losses it means a deterioration. These losses are often known too late to be used as an indicator. Late payment experience, on the other hand, is easier to trace by banks and is mostly a sign of liquidity difficulties. Banks and suppliers should, therefore, register late payments carefully and ascertain their reasons. In only a very few cases are late payments due to technical difficulties. A last sign of liquidity problems might be the utilisation of International Monetary Fund credits or quotas. This can indicate to what degree a country's financial situation has deteriorated, because it now depends on IMF credits. It will, on the other hand, have to adhere to the conditions imposed by the International Monetary Fund.

Current account balance/GNP ratio

With this ratio it is possible to focus more on the medium-term performance of a country's external situation in relation to its gross national product. Account should therefore be taken not only of one year but possibly three years, namely the current, the preceding and the following one. The equation would read as follows:

$$\text{Ratio} = \frac{\dfrac{x\,(n-1)}{y\,(n-1)} + \dfrac{xn}{yn} + \dfrac{x\,(n+1)}{y\,(n+1)}}{3}$$

x = current account balance
y = gross national product
n = current year

For the current and forthcoming years it would obviously be necessary to depend on estimates. They add a certain inexactitude which is, however, largely discounted through the averaging. While a positive ratio is a sign of at least a balanced situation, a negative ratio forces the country in question to obtain outside funds or use its reserves. A minus 5 per cent ratio indicates already a fairly difficult situation, depending on the use of the funds.

Growth-of-export ratio

Because transfer risk is in direct relation to availability of the necessary foreign exchange, the growth rate of the normally most important factor for such availability, namely exports, should also be considered. An economy which is able to enjoy continuous growth in exports, i.e. in volumes of exports, is internationally competitive. It can also be assumed that such an economy has the capability of adjusting to a changing environment. As with some of the other ratios referred to, this ratio should be averaged by taking into account the growth rate over several years. Some examples of major countries and their yearly average export growth rates, using US dollar f.o.b. figures, are as follows:

	1980–85
Brazil	+4.6%
United Kingdom	−1.4%
South Korea	+8.9%
Nigeria	−8.4%
Japan	+6.2%

Countries with ratios of over 5 per cent average real export growth can be considered good performers in international markets. When talking about export performance, a country's export structure must also be considered in some detail. A diversified structure that grows is always better than reliance on a few commodities. From a review of a country's export structure, a so-called commodity reliance factor can be constructed, which will indicate to what extent the country in question is dependent on one or very few commodities or services to earn its foreign exchange. Besides oil, agricultural commodities and tourism, remittances from workers abroad must also be looked at. A fairly high dependence on one source would mean an additional risk coming from that side. The case of oil is probably the only example where it is still assumed that dependence is more of an opportunity than a risk.

Compressibility ratio

This ratio assumes that imports can always be compressed to a certain extent in order to save foreign exchange. The import side is, therefore, analysed and divided into basic needs: energy, raw materials, investment goods and luxury goods. While the last category can be eliminated fairly easily from the list of imported goods by the government of a country in financial difficulties, basic needs always have to be covered. It is hard for an outsider to measure the compressibility ratio, but in most cases it can be assumed that a country in difficulty can compress its imports by about 25 per cent without too much harm. It probably cannot sustain such a compression over a long period of time since shortages in some sectors will certainly develop and, therefore, add a counter-productive effect. This has lately been the case in Poland, where the absence of spare parts due to foreign exchange shortage has halted or slowed down production in several sectors of the economy.

Spread analysis

Spread analysis has also been viewed as a method to evaluate transfer risk. This method takes its justification from the reasoning that the largest part of international cross-border debt is incurred in international financial markets. It is then argued that the prices made in these markets – which are basically the spreads and fees – are very good risk indicators as they show, through their differentiations, the acceptability of a risk by a large number of market participants. In order to use spread analysis, compatibility has to be found in the credits and capital market transactions that are to be analysed. The transactions must have the same type of borrower, which excludes the comparison of private borrowers but limits the analysis essentially to sovereign risks. Furthermore, it is necessary that the transactions have the same length and that they have been signed roughly at the same date in order to be comparable. In addition, the fee structure of the transaction must be incorporated in the spread. This limits the number of transactions that are actually comparable and thus makes the method a very coarse one – a major drawback of such an analysis.

Spread analysis further implies that the market is a better judge of transfer risk than the country risk analyst. This is at least debatable. Spread analysis seems to overrate the influence of the market to a certain extent. It is also extremely difficult to find comparable situations over a lengthy period of time to justify this procedure. Spread analysis, therefore, often compares isolated operations. It can be useful as an additional factor when evaluating country risk. The Euromoney country rating relies heavily on spread analysis.

Logit analysis

The method of using logit analysis[1] to assess country risk has been originally developed by G. Feder and R. E. Just. Their model tries to forecast the probability of a rescheduling in a specific year. It is based on an extensive study of rescheduling operations in the late 1960s and early 1970s. It uses 21 observations on defaults from 11 countries. In addition, it takes into account 217 non-default cases during the period 1965–72. The sample was very representative as it included 238 observations from 41 countries which at that time accounted for 85 per cent of the total outstanding debt for all developing countries. The model reverts to the major economic indicators that are still used today in transfer risk assessment. The seven indicators which were tested are all available from sources such as the World Bank and the International Monetary Fund, as well as the United Nations *Statistical Year Book*. Analysed were the debt service ratio, the import/reserves ratio, the amortisation/debt ratio, income per capita, capital inflow, GNP per capita growth and export growth. Logit analysis stipulates that an eventual correlation between, for example, the debt service ratio and the probability of default or rescheduling can be approximated by a curve like L, which relates probability values between zero and unity to the values of the debt service ratio observed (o) in the sample chosen – as illustrated in Fig. 6.1.

In mathematical terms, it is postulated that the probability of default (Y) is a logistical function of the debt service ratio (x):

$$Y = \frac{e^{\beta x}}{1 + e^{\beta x}}$$

1. Feder, G. and Just, R. E., *Journal of Development Economics*, 3/1977. 'A Study of Debt Servicing Capacity Applying Logit Analysis'.

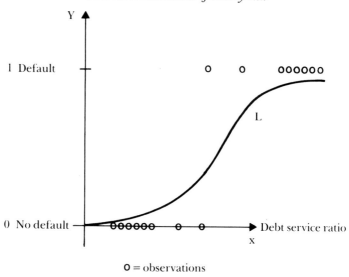

O = observations

Fig. 6.1. Probability curve of default

where β determines the specific form of the L curve. β can be established empirically through a maximum likelihood procedure. The method can be expanded by simultaneously estimating logit coefficients for different economic indicators, using a stepwise procedure. The authors tested four

Table 6.3. Logit estimates of default probability

Variable	Case			
	(a)	(b)	(c)	(d)
Debt service ratio	53.6619	59.2085	35.9826	38.0096
	(2.5731)	(3.2864)	(3.3768)	(3.6181)
Imports/reserves	0.3946	0.3867	0.3614	0.3535
	(1.8323)	(1.7877)	(1.8622)	(1.7895)
Amortisation/debt	−34.6172	−39.6368		
	(1.6535)	(2.1808)		
Income/capita	−0.0116	−0.0124	−0.0113	−0.0142
	(2.4708)	(2.8337)	(3.0333)	(3.5523)
Capital inflow/	−2.6685	−2.8591	−2.1301	−2.2730
debt service	(2.9576)	(3.3930)	(3.4862)	(3.6666)
GDP growth	−18.1495		−50.3238	
	(0.4011)		(1.4274)	
Export growth	−44.8634	−52.6046	−30.5812	−47.3640
	(1.7120)	(2.7077)	(1.6159)	(2.8498)
Likelihood ratio index	0.9222	0.9217	0.9086	0.9019
Likelihood ratio statistic	304.2605	304.0954	299.7940	297.5613

Note: Figures in parentheses denote *t*-values.

cases, with coefficient estimates as indicated in Table 6.3 (respective test values for their significance in parentheses).

Columns (a), (b), (c) and (d) include logit estimates for different combinations of economic indicators. On statistical grounds, cases (b) and (c) seem to be the most reliable ones.

In order to obtain the probability estimate for a specific country of default, the values of the different economic indicators would have to be multiplied by the logit estimates, using the following formula:

$$Y = \frac{e^{\beta_1 x_1 + \beta_2 x_2 + \beta_3 x_3 + \ldots}}{1 + e^{\beta_1 x_1 + \beta_2 x_2 + \beta_3 x_3 + \ldots}}$$

β_1 = logit estimate for variable debt service ratio
x_1 = debt service ratio of country chosen
β_2 = logit estimate for variable import/reserve ratio
x_2 = import/reserve ratio of country chosen
β_3 = logit estimate for variable export growth
x_3 = export growth ratio of country chosen

Through similar calculations one obtains for each country analysed a value between 0 and 1, 1 being the case of default and 0 the case of non-default. Given a critical value of the probability for rescheduling (P^*), all countries with a greater probability would be denied credit while all the others would still enjoy creditworthiness. Under such an assumption two types of error are possible, namely that a country with a lower probability than P^* did default (Type I) or that a country with a higher probability than P^* did not default (Type II). In no case of P^* were more than 11 errors made in a total of 238 observations, as indicated in Table 6.4.

Table 6.4. Type I and type II errors based on the logit estimates

	Case (b)		Case (c)	
P^*	Number of Type I errors	Number of Type II errors	Number of Type I errors	Number of Type II errors
0.10	0	10	0	11
0.20	0	6	1	8
0.30	1	6	2	7
0.40	1	5	3	6
0.50	2	4	4	6
0.60	3	4	4	2
0.70	5	1	5	1
0.80	5	1	6	1
0.90	7	1	8	1

If we take a relatively high P^*, Type II errors are rare whereas Type I errors are significant. If P^* is small we find the reverse. An optimum has, therefore, to be found. With a value of 0.65 and higher there is a good chance that a country will have to reschedule in the coming year.

The logit analysis approach to transfer risk assessment is used today by several banks, which have further developed the model by changing some of the indicators and, therefore, by reviewing the logit estimates. It seems from recent experience that the results obtained through the logit analysis approach are quite encouraging. The use of logit analysis requires professional economic staff as well as the necessary computer equipment.

Assessment of transfer risk

While the assessment of political risk is possible in many different ways, the assessment of transfer risk does not leave such a wide choice. This is because of the much clearer relation between the risk and the factors influencing it. Some methods have already been described. There is, however, still room for the qualitative as well as quantitative method, because the factors that influence the flow of foreign exchange are only seldom quantifiable, whereas the indicators are much more easily so.

Furthermore, the aim of the transfer risk assessment must be established. Should it focus as an early warning system on the short-term capability of a country to service its debt, or rather on obtaining through the assessment an indication of the general development of a country's situation? It might not be possible to obtain, through a specific way of assessing transfer risk, an answer to both questions. The assessment system has to be chosen, to a certain extent, according to whether it is the liquidity aspect that is its primary object or the solvency aspect. Having long-term commitments in a country would probably lead in the first place to a system that tries to give a fair indication of the development of the country's solvency and that identifies fundamental economic problems. If one is on the short end of commitments as an exporter of consumer goods, it is the liquidity aspect that is of prime interest.

The assessment of transfer risk can be done by constructing an index through which the country is rated. Normally a scale of 1–100 is used. Within this scale the very low risk country reaches a high number of points, whereas the extremely high risk countries are on the low end of the scale. To each factor or indicator used is attributed a specific weight or points. Within the range of the weight or points, the better performer obtains a higher result than the medium or low performer, as shown in Table 6.5.

Through the addition of each individual factor or indicator, the position of a country within the index is obtained. If it is decided to limit the assessment to the computation of statistics and, therefore, to a pure quantitative approach, the assessment can be done by anybody who has

The economic element

Table 6.5. Transfer risk – factor: inflation

Most recent year	Weight 5 per cent
Below 5 per cent	10
5–10 per cent	8
10–20 per cent	5
20–40 per cent	2
Above 40 per cent	0

access to the right statistical data. The important work then lies only in the elaboration of the best mix of data and its corresponding weighting to structure the index. It is, however, preferable that the transfer risk assessment also contains a qualitative part. This is because policies regarding the management of the economy cannot be measured in a quantitative way, but are nonetheless very important for the economic well-being of a country. Furthermore, the time lag between assessment and availability of statistical data often calls for qualitative assessment. The use of statistical data only gives, in addition, a fairly one-eyed view. A pure qualitative approach to assessing transfer risk is not desirable either because statistical data are available in one form or another and can, therefore, help to improve the quality of the assessment. Moreover, every qualitative statement would certainly find part of its justification in an analysis of available data; it would thus be more meaningful to use the data in the first place instead of assessing it beforehand. In constructing the index one should also bear in mind that only readily available data that are consistent from country to country should be used, which means for the time being a limitation to the standard sources such as the World Bank, International Monetary Fund or Bank for International Settlements.

The solvency aspect

First to be dealt with is assessment of the transfer risk that has its origin in a deterioration of a country's solvency, i.e. the long-term situation of the country. Research based on past reschedulings is, with the exception of some of the findings of logit analysis, not conclusive enough to determine clearly which factors or indicators must be weighted at a certain rate to obtain the curve of transfer risk development and to forecast the date of rescheduling (rescheduling meaning, among other things, a clear deterioration of transfer risk). It has, however, been proved that certain behaviour on the part of a country often leads more rapidly to problems. Such behaviour includes excessive borrowing to finance consumption, excessive credit creation, excessive debt accumulation and weak export growth.

It has also not been possible so far to construct a model incorporating the forecasting of such behaviour, because it seems that deteriorating or

67

improving creditworthiness is not only the result of a change in key economic indicators but also – and very often – the result of an expression of political will through a government, as well as of the judgement of financial markets. This statement should not, however, discourage us from trying through a system of assessment to measure the fever of the patient. It will be up to the institution itself to first determine the major criteria relevant to its commitment to the country in question.

For banks, a combination of both the qualitative and quantitative approaches seems to be the most suitable and also the most widely used method, with a clear selection of the factors and indicators to be used. While through the qualitative approach the management of the economy and related policies can be assessed, the quantitative part of the appraisal would use the economic indicators. Since the different risk factors are then weighted, not only is their selection important, but also the weight assigned to each. The larger the number of factors used, the more difficult will be the weighting because each factor will contribute only a small percentage to the total and, therefore, the influence of each will decrease. It is thus suggested that the total number of factors or indicators be divided into three groups, each having a large part of the weighting. Each of the major groups would focus on one particular point that is relevant to the development of the country's transfer risk. The three major groups would consist of the indicators relating to debt service capability, management of the economy, and the group of indicators relating to the economy of the country in question. How these three groups are weighted against each other is again a matter of judgement for the institution concerned.

John K. Thompson[1] proposes nine indicators, the weight of 45 per cent of which is assigned to indicators relating to debt service capability. He uses three indicators focusing mainly on exports, as will be seen in Table 6.6.

J. N. Robinson[1] in his assessment format (see Table 6.7) uses 11 indicators that relate to debt service capability. Measuring only economic considerations, those 11 indicators have a weight of 46 per cent.

Debt service capability, i.e. in essence the capability of earning the necessary foreign exchange, must in any rating system assume the major weight when we try to measure the solvency of a country. The choice of the group of indicators to do that depends on the ratios available, but should in any case include the debt service ratio, the debt/GNP ratio and the interest service ratio. If possible, it would be very valuable to use indicators that also incorporate a forward-looking component. For some of the ratios, forward projections exist.

The second group of indicators would deal with the management of the

1. Thompson, John K., *Euromoney*, July 1981.
1. Robinson, J. N., *The Banker*, January 1981.

Table 6.6. Indicators used in structural index

Indicator	Weight %
1. Per cent change in consumer prices:	
(a) most recent year	5
(b) five-year average	5
(c) most recent year/five-year average	5
2. Per cent change in money supply (M1) 1 year/	
per cent change in real GDP (five-year average)	10
3. Change in central bank financing of government/	
monetary base (most recent year)	5
4. Purchasing power parity	5
5. Growth of exports	
(a) most recent year	10
(b) four-year average	10
6. Exports/GDP (most recent year)	10
7. Debt/exports (most recent year)	15
8. Savings/GDP (four-year average)	10
9. Growth of real per capita GDP (five-year average)	10

Note: GDP (gross domestic product) = GNP minus transactions with other countries.

economy. This part of the assessment could be done purely on a quantitative basis, but qualitative parameters such as quality of monetary policy, development policy or currency parity policy should, preferably, also be introduced. The weight of management of the economy needs to be increased in the index if the forward-looking aspect of the assessment is of importance. This is especially true if we evaluate a country that is currently in a rescheduling process. In such a case it is no longer debt service capability that is of major importance when assessing the creditworthiness of the country, but rather the quality of the management of its economy.

The third major group will deal with the indicators relating to the economy of the country concerned. Such indicators would be, for example, GNP per head of population, the consumer price index, GNP growth and natural resources. These indicators are certainly important when we talk about the solvency of a country in the longer-term context. They are, however, of less significance than the two groups of indicators already mentioned. In order to be of greater relevance, these indicators should always take into account the estimates made for the coming years.

A weighting of 50 per cent for debt service capability indicators, 35 per cent for the management of the economy and 15 per cent for the economy would give a balanced view of transfer risk in relation to the solvency of the country concerned.

The review of transfer risk in relation to the solvency of the country concerned should be made once a year, i.e. when most of the statistical data for the previous year are available (which means, at the earliest, in the

Table 6.7. An assessment format

	Approximate weighting (%)	
1. Legal considerations		10
2. Political considerations		25
3. Economic considerations:		
– Power of the government (e.g. a Danish-type minority government which finds it difficult to introduce unpopular measures compared with a British first-past-the-post system)		6
– Assessment of current plans for the economy; feasibility of development plans, main bottlenecks, etc.; resource base – natural and human resources, etc.		15
– Recent events and present state of the economy		
GNP growth	0.3	
Rate of inflation	0.6	
Government budget position	0.6	
Money supply growth	0.3	
Current account balance of payments	0.3	
Unemployment	0.6	
Level of external debt	1.2	
Debt service ratio	1.2	
Latest date of published statistics	0.9	
		6
– Future prospects for the economy if present trends and policies continue		
GNP growth	0.7	
Rate of inflation	1.3	
Government budget position	2.0	
Money supply growth	0.7	
Current account balance of payments	2.0	
Unemployment	1.3	
Level of external debt	2.5	
Debt service ratio	2.5	
		13
– Ability of the country to correct adverse implications of present binds and to withstand unforeseen shocks (vulnerability)		
Imports as a proportion of GDP	0.7	
Exports as a proportion of GDP	0.7	
Diversification of imports by category and by geographical area	4.6	
Diversification of exports by category and by geographical area	4.6	
Compressibility of imports (i.e. extent to which imports consist of 'non-essentials')	6.4	
Vulnerability of the economy to changing prices of main exports and imports; energy dependence	8.0	
		25
		100

second half of each year). As considerable importance is attached to the management of the economy, a change in government policy should also lead to a reassessment of the country concerned. The qualitative aspects that must be reviewed in the assessment of transfer risk are best dealt with by country specialists and international economists.

The liquidity aspect

Recent experience with debt rescheduling has shown that the liquidity aspects in evaluating transfer risk are becoming more and more important. The liquidity situation is influenced by the short-term performance of the country on its external balance and by the management of its foreign debt, and depends on seasonal factors. A further important influence comes, however, from outside the country: the performance of financial markets in relation to different countries. Certainly some of the reschedulings of the past were due mainly to that behaviour.

As already mentioned, the liquidity aspects of transfer risk are much more difficult to evaluate because the data needed to evaluate them are often not obtainable in time. In addition, short-term debt data on many countries are not available at all. The non-availability of such data should not, however, lead to an abandon of the search for a pertinent assessment of the short-term end of transfer risk. John K. Thompson[1] has constructed a liquidity index, set out in Table 6.8.

Table 6.8. Indicators used in liquidity index

Indicator	Weight
1. Reserves/imports	40
2. Debt service/exports	20
3. Large reserve losses	10
4. Late payment experience	10
5. IMF credit/quota	20

In this index the greatest weight is given to the reserves/imports ratio, assuming that a certain number of months of imports could be covered by the reserves when exports are no longer possible. The index does not measure the short-term aspects of country indebtedness, which have become increasingly important, especially for the newly industrialised countries. Only the very poor countries still do not rely on the short-term interbank money market. It seems that this interbank market aspect should be measured in one way or another. The liquidity gap ratio is probably the best indicator to measure the short-term aspect of transfer risk. Together

1. Thompson, John K., *Euromoney*, July 1981.

with an import coverage or reserves/imports ratio, these indicators could best evaluate the major aspects of the liquidity side of transfer risk assessment.

Late payment experience, as indicated in John K. Thompson's liquidity index, is already a sign of a seriously affected situation unless evidence can show that technical problems alone are the basis of the problem. Furthermore, late payment experience may be patchy, since a country can make a selection for its payments, delaying payments only to a specific group of creditors without the other group of creditors knowing it. Such a differentiation in payments is a proceeding that is, for companies in most countries, legally not acceptable or even subject to prosecution. As a qualitative part of the liquidity index, a market acceptability rate which would try to measure the interbank market acceptance of a specific country could be introduced. Such a factor can obviously be measured only by banks that have substantial interbank business.

The construction of a liquidity index could, therefore, contain as major elements the liquidity gap ratio, the reserves/imports ratio and late payment experience, as well as a qualitative judgement of market acceptability. Since we are dealing with the short-term end of transfer risk, namely the liquidity aspect, it is necessary to evaluate it more regularly than the solvency index. This is especially true for countries that have already reached the level of moderate risk on the solvency index. It should be done at three months' or even shorter intervals.

The index to measure the development of transfer risk could be a combination that takes into account both the solvency and liquidity aspects. Each institution must evaluate which weight it wants to assign to each of the two aspects.

Country weighting

As countries differ from each other substantially, and as it has been suggested that they fall roughly into five categories, one might ask if for the different countries a different weighting should be used, or even different indicators. With the exception of some Comecon countries, it seems that the same indicators can be used. The weighting between the different parts of the index could, however, vary from one group of countries to another. While the market acceptability rate is of crucial importance for the newly industrialised countries that use the interbank market, it is for the time being of lesser importance for the large industrialised countries.

For the Comecon countries, more of the assessment probably has to be of a qualitative nature than is the case for other countries, because statistics are not available to the same extent. A selection of the statistics to be used must be made. It will also be important to use consistent statistical sources, such as those mentioned in Chapter 3.

A differentiation in the assessment of transfer risk for different countries could be made. If this is not made in the analysis of the assessment results, countries of similar structure should then be grouped together.

7

Summary of the political and economic aspects

We have now seen that the assessment of country risk involves basically two aspects: political and transfer risk. Transfer risk has, further, a solvency aspect and a liquidity aspect. How should these three different aspects be combined in order to obtain a global assessment of a country risk? Several methods have been used.

The overall index

One way of doing it is to combine the three indices in one super index. This method assumes that country risk is to a certain extent dependent on political risk and to another on transfer risk. The weighting of the two aspects is obviously different for different types of cross-border liabilities. An investment in another country will depend more on political risk, while a sovereign loan is more influenced by transfer risk. In the overall index for banking, political risk is often assigned a 30 per cent weight. Within transfer risk, the liquidity part can account for up to 50 per cent of the weight.

The importance of this index has been growing over the past few years. The disadvantage of an overall index is that a change in the position of a country cannot easily be attributed to one factor or the other, unless the details of the index are reviewed. On the other hand, it is a fairly easy method that shows in one number where a country stands according to the assessment process of country risk. It is also the method used by most of the different rating agencies. It is probably an appropriate method where only a very restricted number of indicators and factors are used.

The combined index

With the combined index, the index used for political risk and transfer risk is divided into score groups, each one with a category number. This can mean that an index score of 81 to 100 would correspond to category V and a score of 0 to 20 would fall into category I. Therefore, for the political risk index one would have categories I to V. The same scoring would be made for the transfer risk index, which could be further divided into a solvency and a liquidity risk index.

In order to facilitate the reading of the index, the letters A to E could also be used for political risk. A country would then rate, e.g., A/IV/IV, which would mean a very low political risk and a low transfer risk for the solvency as well as liquidity aspect. Such a combined index is perhaps cruder than the overall index. On the other hand, it gives a better indication of how the different components of country risk rating relate to each other. If there are big discrepancies between the three figures the situation needs attention, as is the case when the figures are all in the higher category of risk. The combined index is a useful one.

The matrix solution

The matrix solution sees a relation between political and transfer risk. It further assumes that the importance of both risks is similar in relation to country risk (see Fig. 7.1).

		Political risk				
		I	II	III	IV	V
Transfer risk	A					
	B					
	C					
	D					
	E					

Fig. 7.1. The matrix solution

75

On the ordinate, political risk is divided into its components, as is transfer risk on the abscissa. Each country has a score for each of these two major aspects of country risk assessment, which is then placed in the respective square. Low risk countries will always be on the upper left side, while high risk countries will remain on the lower right side. The interesting aspect of a matrix is that it is possible to see, at a quick glance, why a country is moving one way or another. As it is not possible to build in a third dimension to take account of the two aspects of transfer risk, the transfer risk index will have to be structured in such a way as to take care of those aspects in view of specific institutions' aims. The matrix solution would appear to be the most interesting way to combine political and transfer risk. A separate matrix can be used for each group of countries.

8

The different country risk ratings by institutions

Country risk ratings have been undertaken by several institutions. Such ratings are available either through subscription or published in a periodical. Different institutions follow different concepts of country risk assessment, and the concepts can be considered more or less sophisticated. These ratings are a valuable instrument for cross-checking one's own assessment.

The BERI Index[1]

The oldest service that provides country risk information is that of the BERI (Business Environment Risk Information) Institute. Its first index was constructed by Professor F. T. Haner in the late 1960s and had, as its objective, the classification of about 50 countries – giving each one a rating between zero and 100, which would represent the political and economic climate of each country. The BERI Institute, under Professor Haner, has since expanded its services and today offers basically three country risk services, namely:

– the original *Beri Index*
– country forecast reports
– forecast of country risk for international lenders (Forelend)

The original *BERI Index* (now called the Business Risk Service) evaluates three components of country risk, namely the business climate for foreigners, political stability, and currency and repayment risk. It currently reviews 48 countries and appears three times a year. The country analysis reports

1. The *Beri Index* is published by BERI SA, 1355 Redondo Avenue, Suite 10, Long Beach, CA 90804, USA.

77

(FORCE) look mainly at the investment climate and other means of profitable business by foreigners in the countries reviewed.

FORCE are designed to provide international banking and business with the perspective needed to anticipate critical political, economic and financial changes in key countries. The reports are 40–60 single pages and include (1) an executive summary, (2) sections entitled Socio-political Forecast, Economic Forecast, Monetary and Financial Conditions and Operating Conditions, and (3) appropriate appendices. Clients are surveyed annually to identify the countries that they prefer for the following year, and 30–32 reports are prepared which give in-depth follow-up to the other services.

The Forelend system evaluates, through qualitative and quantitative assessments, the creditworthiness of a country. It is forecast-orientated since it looks at the future of a country for up to five years. Several quantitative and qualitative criteria are combined. The different criteria are then further combined in three ratings, which added together give the creditworthiness rating of the country analysed. The three ratings are the quantitative, qualitative and environment ratings. The quantitative rating measures and indicates a country's capability to service its foreign public and private debt. It has a weight of 50 per cent in the overall creditworthiness rating, and is based on four subindices which measure foreign exchange earnings, the foreign debt situation, the reserve position and government finances. The various subindices differ in their weight for compilation of the quantitative rating.

The qualitative rating, which has a weight of 25 per cent in the overall rating, looks at the competence of the economic management of the country, the structure of foreign debt (short-term, long-term), the regulations regarding foreign currency transfers, the influence of corruption, and the resolution of the government to meet its foreign obligations. Each of the factors is rated on a scale from one to five and then weighted.

The environment rating, which also has a 25 per cent weighting in the overall rating, reviews the political and social environment prevailing in the country under review, because this environment influences production of the goods exported to service the foreign debt. The environment rating is also divided into three subindices, namely the political risk index, the business climate index and the index on socio-political environment. While the first two subindices are arrived at through the panel method, the third is established by the BERI Institute. For the panel method the Institute consults a number of outside experts, who regularly review all the factors that constitute the subindex.

The three ratings added together then constitute the overall creditworthiness rating or composite score on a scale between 1 and 100. The scale is divided into eight categories of lender ratings, which indicate to the lending

Table 8.1. Forelend Index by BERI SA

Lender's risk ratings ranked by +5 years composite score 1986–III

	Present		+1 year		+5 years	
	LR	Composite score	LR	Composite score	LR	Composite score
1. Singapore	1	75	1	73	1	77
Taiwan (ROC)	1	76	1	74	1	77
3. Norway	1	72	1	69	1	69
4. United Kingdom	1	66	1	65	1	67
5. France	2	61	2	61	1	65
Saudi Arabia	2	61	2	60	1	65
7. Belgium	2	64	2	63	2	64
8. Spain	2	61	2	60	2	62
Sweden	2	61	2	61	2	62
10. Denmark	3	57	3	56	3	55
11. Australia	3	56	4	54	4	53
Canada	3	57	3	55	4	53
Italy	4	53	4	52	4	53
Korea (South)	4	52	4	51	4	53
15. Ireland	4	54	4	54	4	52
16. New Zealand	4	54	4	53	4	51
17. Malaysia	4	50	5	48	4	50
Thailand	4	51	5	49	4	50
Turkey	5	49	5	48	4	50
20. India	5	49	5	49	5	48
Portugal	5	49	5	48	5	48
22. Algeria	5	47	5	45	5	47
23. Colombia	5	49	5	47	5	46
Kenya	5	47	5	46	5	46
South Africa	5	49	5	48	5	46
26. Israel	5	49	5	47	5	45
Pakistan	6	44	6	44	5	45
28. Cameroon	4	50	5	47	6	44
Ivory Coast	5	45	6	44	6	44
30. Paraguay	5	46	5	45	6	43
31. Brazil	6	43	6	41	6	42
Greece	5	47	5	45	6	42
Indonesia	6	43	6	41	6	42
34. Panama	6	42	6	41	6	41
35. Iraq	7	39	7	37	6	40
Zimbabwe	6	44	6	42	6	40
37. Venezuela	6	40	7	38	7	38
38. Chile	7	39	7	38	7	37
Ecuador	7	39	7	36	7	37
40. Argentina	7	36	8	34	7	36
41. Iran	7	37	7	35	7	35
42. Egypt	7	39	7	37	8	34
Jamaica	7	39	7	36	8	34
Nigeria	7	36	8	34	8	34
Peru	8	34	8	33	8	34
46. Mexico	7	37	7	35	8	33
47. Morocco	7	37	7	37	8	32
Philippines	7	35	8	34	8	32
49. Bolivia	8	30	8	29	8	30
Zaire	8	31	8	31	8	30

79

institution the quality of the borrower and suggest a certain behaviour. The Forelend review is published three times a year and covers 50 countries. In addition to the statistical data, a two-page analysis is made for each country covering economic, political and financial development from the lender's point of view. Furthermore, it publishes for each oil-importing country a 'saturation factor' which measures debt service plus imports of petroleum in relation to total foreign exchange earnings. Saturation is reached when that factor rises to 80 per cent. The BERI *Forelend Index* follows classical assessment of country risk and is, therefore, a useful tool for that purpose. Unfortunately, it covers only a selection of countries world-wide. However, the major borrowing countries are included. Table 8.1 shows the Forelend Index as at the end of 1986.

Euromoney country risk rating

The *Euromoney* country risk rating is published annually in *Euromoney*. Its method is based on the performance of a country in the financial markets. The key criteria for ranking are access to the market, the terms actually obtained or, failing that, as assessed by the market, and the selldown, which means the success of the operation. The markets considered include the bond markets, from Yankee bonds to Eurobonds, the floating rate note market (FRNs), revolving underwriting facilities and bankers' acceptances. All the facets of the Euronote and Euroloan market are also considered.

The rating includes the syndicated loan market with LIBOR (London Interbank Offered Rate), prime pricing as well as certificates of deposit (CDs) options, club deals and specific bank-to-bank loans. Furthermore, the *à forfait* market as quoted by the secondary market makers or by market judgement is analysed. Trade financing is also reviewed in order to obtain an idea as to what type of trade finance a country has access to, such as letters of credit with cash against documents or cash in advance. The rankings, once they have been compiled, are shown to political risk insurers and top syndicate managers in the Euromarket for their comments. In 1986 the weighting was as follows:

- Political risk   20 per cent
- Access to market   20 per cent
- Access to trade finance   10 per cent
  (forfaiting)
- Payment record   15 per cent
  (whether on time or late)
- Selldown   30 per cent
- Difficulties in rescheduling 5 per cent

For each of the 119 countries rated, a score was established as well as a rank.

Institutional Investor's country credit rating

The *Institutional Investor* publishes biannually a country credit rating based on a survey undertaken together with some 75–100 internationally operating banks. The banks are asked to rate each country on a scale from zero to 100, with zero representing the least creditworthy countries and those with the greatest chances of default, and 100 representing the most creditworthy and those with the least chances of default. The individual responses are weighted using an *Institutional Investor* formula that gives more weight to responses from banks with the largest world-wide exposure and the most sophisticated country analysis system. Due to its sources, the *Institutional Investor*'s country credit rating gives a fair image of the status of a country within the international banking community. Table 8.2 shows a comparison of autumn 1986 *Euromoney* and *Institutional Investor* country credit rating.

Table 8.2. Institutional Investor and Euromoney credit rating, autumn 1986

	Institutional Investor[1]		Euromoney[2]	
	Rank	Score	Rank	Score
Japan	1	95.7	1	100
United States	2	95.1	1	100
Switzerland	3	94.5	1	100
West Germany	4	94.2	1	100
United Kingdom	5	87.5	1	100
The Netherlands	6	87.4	1	100
Canada	7	87.1	9	98
France	8	83.9	13	94
Norway	9	83.5	10	97
Austria	10	83.3	11	95
Australia	11	80.1	16	92
Sweden	12	79.4	1	100
Finland	13	78.0	17	87
Belgium	14	76.5	1	100
Italy	15	76.1	21	83
Singapore	16	74.5	30	68
Taiwan	17	73.9	30	68
Denmark	18	73.4	11	95
Spain	19	70.4	19	84
Hong Kong	20	69.4	23	75
New Zealand	21	68.2	15	93
China	22	68.1	22	78

1. *Institutional Investor*, September 1986.
2. *Euromoney*, September 1986.

81

Table 8.2. – cont.

	Institutional Investor		Euromoney	
	Rank	Score	Rank	Score
USSR	23	66.7	19	84
Saudi Arabia	24	64.9	36	65
Ireland	25	64.6	18	86
Kuwait	26	62.3	38	63
Malaysia	27	59.9	36	65
United Arab Emirates	28	58.6	43	57
South Korea	29	58.4	25	73
Bahrain	30	56.1	35	66
East Germany	31	55.8	33	67
Qatar	32	54.2	27	70
Thailand	33	53.3	39	62
Czechoslovakia	34	53.1	33	67
Oman	35	52.7	47	52
Iceland	36	52.1	24	74
Portugal	37	51.8	26	71
Hungary	38	51.3	28	69
India	39	50.7	28	69
Algeria	40	50.4	44	55
Bulgaria	41	49.6	40	61
Greece	42	47.6	41	60
Indonesia	43	47.6	42	59
Trinidad and Tobago	44	43.3	66	38
South Africa	45	40.6	60	41
Gabon	46	40.4	56	43
Tunisia	47	39.7	47	52
Colombia	48	39.2	59	42
Papua New Guinea	49	39.2	50	51
Cyprus	50	39.0	47	52
Turkey	51	38.6	45	54
Cameroon	52	38.4	71	36
Venezuela	53	38.1	77	31
Jordan	54	37.7	46	53
Brazil	55	35.2	73	35
Barbados	56	33.2	50	51
Romania	57	32.0	63	39
Yugoslavia	58	31.4	82	29
Panama	59	31.0	56	43
Paraguay	60	31.0	77	31
Israel	61	30.9	60	41
Mexico	62	30.8	77	31
Pakistan	63	29.8	52	50
Kenya	64	29.8	66	38
Egypt	65	29.5	56	43

The different country risk ratings by institutions

Table 8.2 – cont.

	Institutional Investor		Euromoney	
	Rank	Score	Rank	Score
Uruguay	66	27.8	86	28
Ivory Coast	67	27.5	87	27
Libya	68	27.3	98	21
Ecuador	69	26.7	80	30
Chile	70	25.1	98	21
Argentina	71	24.9	82	29
Mauritius	72	24.9	62	40
Sri Lanka	73	24.6	63	39
Morocco	74	23.1	82	29
Zimbabwe	75	23.1	74	34
Nigeria	76	22.8	109	17
Philippines	77	21.4	92	25
Syria	78	19.7	66	38
Iran	79	19.3	117	10
Senegal	80	18.6	94	23
Iraq	81	18.2	103	20
Malawi	82	18.1	93	24
Bangladesh	83	18.0	108	18
Costa Rica	84	17.0	97	22
Congo	85	15.8	75	33
Poland	86	15.4	70	37
Peru	87	14.9	98	21
Jamaica	88	14.9	80	30
Dominican Republic	89	14.5	94	23
Cuba	90	14.2	82	29
Angola	91	13.6	89	26
Guatemala	92	13.2	94	23
Honduras	93	12.9	116	13
Seychelles	94	12.2	–	–
Zambia	95	11.0	103	20
Liberia	96	11.0	–	–
Ethiopia	97	10.8	113	16
Tanzania	98	10.8	87	27
Lebanon	99	10.2	103	20
Zaire	100	9.9	98	21
Haiti	101	9.6	113	16
Bolivia	102	8.0	113	16
Grenada	103	8.0	–	–
El Salvador	104	7.4	118	6
Sudan	105	7.3	118	6
Sierra Leone	106	7.2	–	–
North Korea	107	5.6	–	–
Nicaragua	108	5.5	–	–
Uganda	109	5.1	109	17

Euromoney has in addition rated the following countries: Botswana, Burma, Fiji, Ghana, Guyana, Lesotho, Luxembourg, Malta, Mauritania, Mozambique, Nauru, Niger, Solomon Islands and Swaziland.

A comparison between the two rankings shows some interesting results. Within the first 20 rankings it is remarkable how the two institutions arrive at different ratings, such as Belgium, Denmark, Italy, Singapore and Sweden. It is also interesting to see that of the Latin American countries, the *Institutional Investor* rates Brazil, Chile and Venezuela substantially better than *Euromoney*. The *Institutional Investor* ranking is based mainly on the country rating system of major banks, while the *Euromoney* rating is more market-orientated. As banks are the major participants in the market, there seems to be some divergence between the ratings of the banking system and its behaviour in the markets.

International Country Risk Guide[1]

The *International Country Risk Guide* (*ICRG*) is also a country risk assessment system which rates each country with a specific score. It is published on a monthly basis. *ICRG* arrives at its scoring by breaking down the total score into three components, which cover the political, financial and economic risks. The political variable contributes 50 per cent to the score and the financial and economic indicators 25 per cent each. The assessment of political risk is based on 13 indicators which together add up to 100 points. Indicators such as political leadership, law and order tradition, and quality of bureaucracy are some of the factors used. Five indicators have been identified to assess financial risk and cover such factors as loan default or unfavourable loan restructuring, losses from foreign exchange controls, and repudiation of contracts by governments. The five indicators add up to 50 points. Economic risk is assessed through six indicators, such as inflation, debt service ratio and international liquidity, and adds another 50 points. The scoring is then obtained by the following formula:

CPFER (country X) = 0.5 (PF + FF + EF)
CPFER   = Composite political, financial and economic rating

PF = Total political indicators
FF = Total financial indicators
EF = Total economic indicators

The scores can range from 0 (highest risk) to 100 (lowest risk). They are, furthermore, classified into the broad categories of very high risk, moderately high risk, moderate risk, low risk and very low risk.

1. The *International Country Risk Guide* is published by the International Reports Group, 200 Park Avenue South, New York, NY 1003, USA.

In addition, each month the issue covers some countries in more detail and shows the development of the rating of that country in a graph.

As the *ICRG* weights political risk with 50 per cent in its total scoring, countries with a stable political climate but a not so immaculate economic situation obtain in general better rating than in the *Institutional Investor* or *Euromoney* rating. The *ICRG* is a valuable tool in country risk assessment; its composite rating as of March 1987 is given in Table 8.3.

Table 8.3. International Country Risk Guide, composite risk rating, March 1987

	Mar. 1987 Composite political financial and economic risk rating	Feb. 1987 Composite political financial and economic risk rating	Nov./Dec. 1986 Composite political financial and economic risk rating	Mar. 1987 v. Feb. 1987	Mar. 1987 v. Nov./Dec. 1986
Albania	62.0	62.5	62.5	−0.5	−0.5
Algeria	54.0	54.5	55.0	−0.5	−1.0
Angola	46.0	46.0	44.0	0.0	2.0
Argentina	43.0	43.0	42.0	0.0	1.0
Australia	76.5	76.5	77.0	0.0	−0.5
Austria	85.0	84.5	83.5	0.5	1.5
Bahamas	72.0	72.0	72.0	0.0	0.0
Bahrain	61.5	61.5	61.0	0.0	0.5
Bangladesh	39.0	39.0	39.0	0.0	0.0
Belgium	82.0	81.0	81.0	1.0	1.0
Bolivia	33.5	33.5	30.5	0.0	3.0
Botswana	68.0	68.0	67.5	0.0	0.5
Brazil	54.0	55.5	54.5	−1.5	−0.5
Brunei	81.0	81.0	81.5	0.0	−0.5
Bulgaria	62.5	63.0	62.0	−0.5	0.5
Burkina Faso	51.0	50.5	50.5	0.5	0.5
Burma	39.5	40.0	40.0	−0.5	−0.5
Cameroon	59.5	59.0	57.5	0.5	2.0
Canada	82.5	82.5	82.0	0.0	0.5
Chile	51.0	49.5	49.0	1.5	2.0
China, PR	64.5	65.0	65.0	−0.5	−0.5
Colombia	59.5	59.5	59.5	0.0	0.0
Congo	51.5	51.5	51.5	0.0	0.0
Costa Rica	57.0	57.0	58.0	0.0	−1.0
Cuba	47.5	48.0	49.5	−0.5	−2.0
Cyprus	62.5	62.5	62.0	0.0	0.5
Czechoslovakia	71.0	71.5	71.0	−0.5	0.0
Denmark	83.0	84.5	85.0	−1.5	−2.0
Dominican Rep.	50.0	50.0	49.5	0.0	0.5
Ecuador	50.5	51.0	51.0	−0.5	−0.5
Egypt	40.5	40.0	40.0	0.5	0.5
El Salvador	36.5	37.0	37.5	−0.5	−1.0
Ethiopia	39.0	38.5	38.5	0.5	0.5
Finland	84.0	83.0	84.0	1.0	0.0

Table 8.3. – cont.

	Mar. 1987 Composite political financial and economic risk rating	Feb. 1987 Composite political financial and economic risk rating	Nov./Dec. 1986 Composite political financial and economic risk rating	Mar. 1987 v. Feb. 1987	Mar. 1987 v. Nov./Dec. 1986
France	80.0	79.0	78.5	1.0	1.5
Gabon	64.5	64.5	63.5	0.0	1.0
Gambia, The	51.0	51.5	50.0	−0.5	1.0
Germany, DR	68.0	68.5	70.5	−0.5	−2.5
Germany, FR	90.0	89.5	90.0	0.5	0.0
Ghana	48.0	47.5	47.5	0.5	0.5
Greece	59.0	57.5	56.5	1.5	2.5
Guatemala	38.0	38.0	37.5	0.0	0.5
Guinea	46.0	45.0	45.0	1.0	1.0
Guinea-Bissau	38.0	38.0	37.5	0.0	0.5
Guyana	38.5	38.5	38.0	0.0	0.5
Haiti	40.0	40.0	40.0	0.0	0.0
Honduras	44.0	44.0	44.0	0.0	0.0
Hong Kong	77.0	77.0	76.5	0.0	0.5
Hungary	66.0	67.0	66.5	−1.0	−0.5
Iceland	81.0	79.5	78.5	1.5	2.5
India	56.5	57.0	57.0	−0.5	−0.5
Indonesia	47.5	47.5	47.0	0.0	0.5
Iran	35.0	35.0	35.5	0.0	−0.5
Iraq	29.0	29.0	29.5	0.0	−0.5
Ireland	77.0	77.0	78.0	0.0	−1.0
Israel	55.0	55.5	55.5	−0.5	−0.5
Italy	80.0	80.5	80.0	−0.5	0.0
Ivory Coast	66.0	66.0	65.0	0.0	0.5
Jamaica	50.5	50.5	50.0	0.0	0.5
Japan	89.5	89.5	90.0	0.0	−0.5
Jordan	53.0	53.0	53.0	0.0	0.0
Kenya	57.5	57.5	57.5	0.0	0.0
Korea, DPR	60.0	60.5	60.5	−0.5	−0.5
Korea, Rep.	65.5	66.0	65.0	−0.5	0.5
Kuwait	58.0	58.0	58.0	0.0	0.0
Lebanon	29.5	29.5	30.3	0.0	−0.5
Liberia	33.0	33.0	33.0	0.0	0.0
Libya	39.5	39.5	39.5	0.0	0.0
Luxembourg	90.0	89.5	90.0	0.5	0.0
Madagascar	49.5	49.5	49.5	0.0	0.0
Malawi	50.5	51.0	51.0	−0.5	−0.5
Malaysia	63.0	63.0	64.0	0.0	−1.0
Mali	39.0	39.5	39.5	−0.5	−0.5
Malta	65.0	65.0	64.5	0.0	0.5
Mexico	54.0	54.5	54.5	−0.5	−0.5
Mongolia	60.5	60.5	60.5	0.0	0.0
Morocco	45.5	45.5	44.0	0.0	1.5
Mozambique	34.5	34.0	33.0	0.5	1.5
Netherlands	90.0	90.0	90.0	0.0	0.0
New Caledonia	43.5	43.5	44.0	0.0	−0.5

The different country risk ratings by institutions

Table 8.3. – cont.

	Mar. 1987 Composite political financial and economic risk rating	Feb. 1987 Composite political financial and economic risk rating	Nov./Dec. 1986 Composite political financial and economic risk rating	Mar. 1987 v. Feb. 1987	Mar. 1987 v. Nov./Dec. 1986
New Zealand	83.5	82.5	82.5	1.0	1.0
Nicaragua	26.5	26.5	26.0	0.0	0.5
Niger	53.0	53.0	53.0	0.0	0.0
Nigeria	42.0	42.0	42.5	0.0	−0.5
Norway	84.0	86.0	86.5	−2.0	−2.5
Oman	58.0	58.0	57.0	0.0	1.0
Pakistan	48.5	48.5	49.5	0.0	−1.0
Panama	54.0	54.0	54.0	0.0	0.0
Papua New Guinea	65.0	65.0	64.5	0.0	0.5
Paraguay	50.5	50.0	49.0	0.5	1.5
Peru	38.0	38.0	38.5	0.0	−0.5
Philippines	47.0	46.5	48.0	0.5	−1.0
Poland	44.5	45.0	45.0	−0.5	−0.5
Portugal	72.5	72.5	72.5	0.0	0.0
Qatar	55.0	55.5	56.0	−0.5	−1.0
Romania	47.0	47.5	48.0	−0.5	−1.0
Saudi Arabia	55.5	55.5	54.5	0.0	1.0
Senegal	56.0	56.0	56.5	0.0	−0.5
Sierra Leone	47.5	48.0	48.0	−0.5	−0.5
Singapore	77.5	77.5	77.5	0.0	0.0
Somalia	39.5	40.0	40.0	−0.5	−0.5
South Africa	50.5	51.5	51.5	−1.0	−1.0
Soviet Union	65.5	65.5	64.5	0.0	1.0
Spain	75.5	75.5	76.0	0.0	−0.5
Sri Lanka	44.5	44.5	44.5	0.0	0.0
Sudan	31.5	31.5	31.0	0.0	0.5
Surinam	44.5	45.0	45.0	−0.5	−0.5
Sweden	86.0	84.5	84.5	1.5	1.5
Switzerland	94.0	94.0	94.0	0.0	0.0
Syria	41.0	41.0	41.5	0.0	−0.5
Taiwan	81.0	80.5	81.5	0.5	−0.5
Tanzania	47.0	46.5	46.0	0.5	1.0
Thailand	60.5	60.0	60.0	0.5	0.5
Togo	50.5	51.0	50.5	−0.5	0.0
Trinidad	55.5	55.0	56.0	0.5	−0.5
Tunisia	47.5	46.5	46.5	1.0	1.0
Turkey	53.0	53.0	52.5	0.0	0.5
Uganda	38.5	38.0	38.5	0.5	0.0
UAE	53.5	53.5	54.0	0.0	−0.5
UK	82.5	81.0	81.0	1.5	1.5
US	85.5	86.5	86.5	−1.0	−1.0
Uruguay	58.5	58.5	58.0	0.0	0.5
Venezuela	56.5	55.5	55.5	1.0	1.0
Vietnam	43.5	44.0	44.0	−0.5	−0.5
Yemen Arab Rep.	45.0	45.5	45.0	−0.5	0.0
Yemen, PDR	49.0	49.0	49.5	0.0	−0.5

87

Table 8.3. – cont.

	Mar. 1987 Composite political financial and economic risk rating	Feb. 1987 Composite political financial and economic risk rating	Nov./Dec. 1986 Composite political financial and economic risk rating	Mar. 1987 *v.* Feb. 1987	Mar. 1987 *v.* Nov./Dec. 1986
Yugoslavia	49.5	50.0	50.0	−0.5	−0.5
Zaire	37.5	38.0	38.5	−0.5	−1.0
Zambia	44.5	45.5	45.0	−1.0	−0.5
Zimbabwe	47.0	46.5	46.5	0.5	0.5

Part Three
Monitoring of country risk

9

The establishment of country limits

Why a country limit?

It has been standard practice for banks to limit their lending exposures
through the fixing of credit ceilings for their customers. Such credit ceilings
can, however, be structured differently. They are usually divided into lines
of credit for each type of credit a customer of a bank is looking for. The
credit lines are, therefore, structured along a product-orientated system.
They are then normally consolidated for each borrower in order to monitor
the total possible exposure to that client. In a further step, credit lines to the
different companies of a concern can be consolidated. This often has to be
done in accordance with the respective banking laws or supervisory
regulations as well. To look at credit lines not only on a consolidated basis
with regard to the borrower but also to consolidate them by taking into
account all the subsidiaries and majority participations of the lending
institution, is necessary to give a correct picture of the exposure of a bank
towards its customers.

Since banks diversify their risks among different industries and, therefore, like to know the extent of risk diversification, they sometimes also add
together the credit lines available to a specific industry in order to monitor
their exposure to that industry. Such limits are especially important for
banks operating in an economic environment that is dominated by one
industry. Banks might even establish limits for certain sectors of the
economy.

As banks began to realise that cross-border lending involves not only a
credit risk but also a country risk, it became quite obvious that the latter
had to be monitored in order to control the exposure towards a specific

country. The country limit is the instrument used to monitor and control cross-border lending in relation to a particular country and to limit the total exposure to that country. Prudent banking will, therefore, establish country limits for every country where a specific exposure exists or is contemplated.

Analysis of the different cross-border exposures

Cross-border exposure involving a country risk is often of a more complex nature than exposure to a specific client of a bank. It encompasses what one could call direct cross-border exposure and indirect cross-border exposure.

Direct cross-border exposure

Direct cross-border exposure involving a country risk is primarily the exposure to a borrower who has his legal incorporation in the same country as the one where he takes up his loan. This kind of exposure is associated with the term direct country risk. All sovereign borrowing falls into this category. Out of the total amount of cross-border exposure, this part is by far the largest. Direct country risk is also involved in all direct cross-border lending where the borrower takes up his borrowing in a specific country, namely the country of the direct country risk, but does not have his legal incorporation in that country. This kind of cross-border lending can, however, create an indirect cross-border exposure depending on the relation between the borrowing unit and the head office of the parent company. A typical case is the lending to foreign branches of an internationally operating bank. While the credit risk obviously involves the bank as a legal entity, the direct country risk is spread over several countries according to the branch network of the bank.

Direct country risk thus exists only on the cross-border lending of the branch network to a specific country or out of a specific country. If, therefore, the London branch of a major US bank operates within the London market by borrowing from or lending to other participants in that market, it does not incur any direct country risk, although certainly a credit risk. It further involves an indirect country risk if the lending is done to a branch of a foreign bank. The same obviously holds true for a Brazilian branch of a foreign bank that is financing its Brazilian loan portfolio through local deposits. On this loan portfolio no country risk exists for the head office of the bank. However, if an investment in capital is made involving a cross-border transaction, it would have to be accounted for as country risk for the parent company.

It has sometimes been asked whether project financing also falls under the country risk status. An analysis of the origin and kind of pledge of the income stream needed to service the project financing must be made. It then must be decided on a case-by-case basis to which country or countries the country risk should be attributed.

The establishment of country limits

A question that has arisen in this context is the qualification of a direct country risk for the so-called offshore locations or units. Theoretically, lending to offshore locations or units does not involve a country risk but only the credit risk of the borrower involved. This is said under the assumption that the offshore location in its regulation excludes the transfer risk in offshore transactions and is not merely a tax haven classified as offshore. It is advisable to look into the quality of the offshore status and also to qualify such lending as offshore lending. Otherwise a direct country risk might be incurred. Lending to a New York agency of an international bank can involve a New York branch, the International Banking Facility or a Cayman Islands branch.

Direct country risk, therefore, means the cross-border exposure in a specific country where the unit involved as a borrower in the cross-border lending is located. All direct country risk must be accounted for under the country limit established for a specific country.

Indirect cross-border exposure

Indirect cross-border exposure is a by-product of direct cross-border exposure. It is created when there are more than two parties from more than two countries involved in a cross-border transaction. Within the network of such relations we find direct and indirect cross-border exposure. It means that in addition to a direct country risk an indirect country risk is involved. While this leads statistically to double counting, the risks are not added together but stand to each other in an either/or relationship. This must be taken into account when the extent of the country risk is analysed.

The most common transaction involving an indirect country risk is a *guarantee transaction*, where the lending to a borrower in one country is guaranteed by a guarantor in another country. The guarantee must obviously cover credit as well as transfer risk in order to create an indirect country risk. While from a credit risk point of view the credit risk of the guaranteed might often be neglected, it seems unwise to do the same for the transfer risk. The quality of the transfer risk for the country of domicile of the guaranteed can be better than that of the guarantor, whereas for the credit risk normally the reverse holds true. In a guarantee transaction, therefore, the direct country risk lies with the guaranteed and the indirect country risk with the guarantor. The establishment of such an indirect country risk is also called risk transfer.

An exception to this are the cross-border transactions guaranteed by an official export risk guarantee institution. In such a case the funding unit can neglect the direct country risk to the borrower since transfer risk is excluded from the funding transaction through the guarantor. No indirect country risk is created. The main purpose of the export risk guarantee institution is to take over transfer risk from the exporter.

93

Exposures within bank networks

Indirect country risk is also created when we talk about cross-border lending of one bank into the branch network of another bank. The direct country risk is always with the unit taking up the funds because every unit operating in a country is subject to that country's regulation and, therefore, is part of its country risk. An indirect country risk lies with the country of origin of the head office involved through the credit obligation undertaken by the bank as a whole. To this legal aspect is often added the practical aspect when such branches are used as funding units for the home network of the bank involved. As long as we have no internationally acceptable transfer risk clauses that guide banks in qualifying the country risk for branch lending, it is certainly correct to include indirect country risk in monitoring the country risk of the head office of the bank. The indirect country risk within the branch network of banks, i.e. the country risk of the head office, is also called by the lender ultimate country risk.

The importance of such an indirect country risk depends on whether the head office is in a country of very high standing or in one that is considered more risky. The experience with lending to overseas branches of banks where the head office has been involved in a rescheduling exercise confirms such risk assessment. Furthermore, it can happen, say in the case of a London branch, that the supervisory authority where the branch is located asks the head office to establish a letter of intent or even a guarantee in favour of its branch, thus institutionalising the indirect country risk. Banks have, however, notified correspondents in the past that they exclude any liabilities from a materialised transfer risk of their overseas branches, therefore eliminating indirect country risk. Such notification is made when the country risk of the head office is considered to be of better standing than that of the branch office. The case of the Citibank deposits of its Manila branch has highlighted this problem. The legal case that has followed non-payment of part of those deposits has been decided by the United States District Court for the Southern District of New York in May 1987 in favour of the depositor. The court has accepted the use of a bank's worldwide assets to pay the obligations of local branches. Therefore, banks are using appropriate disclaimers in the deposit tickets or confirmation slips.

Another question concerns lending to a subsidiary of a bank or to an institution in a country other than the one where the parent company is located. Under such a construction there is theoretically not even an indirect risk involved, unless there exists a clear support or guarantee agreement not only between parent company and subsidiary, but also one that extends to the lenders to the subsidiary as well. Letters of comfort or awareness certainly do not create an indirect country risk. This being said, however, it can be argued that in practical terms an indirect country risk is nevertheless created, as these institutions often have a very one-sided country exposure towards the country of their origin. Typical examples are many of the Scandinavian banks in Luxembourg. In such cases it is, therefore, advisable to look into the assets side of the institution concerned in order to make a judgement with respect to a possible indirect country risk. Although it might be rather difficult to obtain such information, it is important to assess the potential of such an indirect country risk if the location of the assets is in a country of questionable standing.

Indirect country risk should be included in a country limit in order to have a better picture of the total potential of the cross-border risk incurred. It is a risk similar to the contingent liabilities of a bank. Its importance depends on the importance of the underlying credit transaction. If the underlying guarantee is the basis for the credit transaction, the indirect country risk has nearly the status of a direct country risk. If it stems from the branch borrowing of a major internationally operating bank, the risk is certainly lower. Correspondingly, one can also say that a difference in the quality of the direct and indirect country risks has an implication for the assessment of the latter. The bank will have to evaluate which country risk it can rely on more in order to know the quality of the risks involved.

Foreign exchange risk

Another question that has sometimes been asked is whether there exists a country risk arising from the currency used in cross-border lending. A typical case would be a British bank that lends US dollars to a German borrower. The argument then goes that in such a transaction the United States could block the repayment of the US dollars for one reason or another. Such third-party risk obviously is inherent in many cross-border transactions; it was manifested when the United States froze Iranian assets after the seizure of its embassy and when the United Kingdom froze Argentinian assets during the Falkland Islands war.

This risk is not viewed as a country risk and quite correctly so, because the country risk lies by definition in the relationship between the countries of the borrower and the lender. It is, however, one of the risks involved in international lending and, as described, is a foreign exchange risk. The currencies involved in international cross-border lending are typically the currencies of the major industrialised nations, such as the US dollar, Deutschmark, Dutch guilder, pound sterling, Japanese yen and Swiss franc. Very often these currencies are used in the form of Eurocurrencies. In this case they are not tied to their home market, but have a kind of offshore status. These currencies are also used in international lending because they are considered as always being available. Interference so far has been manifested only under very special circumstances. Furthermore, such interference normally will be neutralised to a large extent because it applies to both sides of the balance sheet.

Lending to supranational institutions

Lending to supranational institutions such as the World Bank, the European Investment Bank, the Nordiska Investerings Bank, the Asian Development Bank, the African Development Bank and others – or to international organisations – does not involve a country risk as long as these institutions enjoy an extraterritorial status. This extraterritoriality frees the institution from the transfer regulations of the country where it is operating. Lending to the supranational institutions, while constituting cross-border lending, involves only the credit risk of the institutions involved. A bank should, therefore, not include these risks in the country risk of the specific country where the institution is located. Nevertheless, it is advisable that the legal status of the supranational institution be looked into and that the responsibilities of the different member states of the institution be checked. As no specific country risk is incurred, the bank might set up a special limit for lending to these institutions, just as it sets up limits for special sectors of the economy.

Size of the country limit

The size of a country limit is the total amount that an institution is willing to take as cross-border exposure towards a specific country. The establishment of that amount is, therefore, of crucial importance for the institution involved. So far there exists no generally agreed rule according to which the size of a country limit can be established. Regulators in most countries leave this up to the management of different institutions. This is very acceptable because it is the management's duty and responsibility to fix the risks it is willing to undertake.

The rescheduling negotiations have shown that some leading international banks were willing to go as high as 80 per cent or more of their equity in lending to certain large Latin American countries in the heydays of international lending. Similar banks have very different exposures to similar countries in relation to their equity.

Based on available information, Table 9.1 shows exposures of certain banks to certain countries in relation to their equity when the restructuring exercises started.

Since then, major changes have occurred as banks had to strengthen their capital basis. Differences still exist and are due to past experiences as well as the ambition with which a bank pursues its international business. Some reflections regarding the size of the country limit should be made. The country limit will have to be based on the consolidated operations of a bank.

Table 9.1. Bank exposure in relation to equity

	(DM or US$ million)		
	Equity*	Exposure	Per cent
Poland			
(non-Hermes-guaranteed)			
Bank für Gemeinwirtschaft	DM1,682	DM780	46.4
Commerzbank	DM2,478	DM600	24.2
Deutsche Bank	DM4,873	DM450	9.2
Dresdner Bank	DM3,365	DM400	11.9
Hessische Landesbank	DM1,241	DM180	14.5
Westdeutsche Landesbank	DM2,850	DM150	5.3
Mexico			
Bank of America	US$4,168	US$2,750	66.0
Citicorp	US$5,485	US$2,725	49.7
Manufacturers Hanover	US$2,110	US$1,730	82.0
Chase Manhattan Bank	US$3,248	US$1,500	46.2
Chemical Bank	US$1,846	US$1,500	81.2
Bankers Trust	US$1,466	US$1,175	80.1
J. P. Morgan	US$2,455	US$1,131	46.1
Brazil			
Citicorp	US$5,485	US$4,360	79.5
Bank of America	US$4,168	US$2,487	59.7
Chase Manhattan Bank	US$3,248	US$2,450	75.4
Manufacturers Hanover	US$2,110	US$2,014	95.5
J. P. Morgan	US$2,455	US$1,752	71.4
Chemical Bank	US$1,846	US$1,300	70.4
Bankers Trust	US$1,466	US$ 775	52.9
Argentina			
Manufacturers Hanover	US$2,110	US$1,230	58.3
Citicorp	US$5,485	US$1,090	19.9
Chase Manhattan Bank	US$3,248	US$ 800	24.6
J. P. Morgan	US$2,455	US$ 761	31.0
Continental Illinois	US$1,779	US$ 383	21.5
Chemical Bank	US$1,846	US$ 372	20.2

Sources: Spiegel, 21 December 1981; *American Banker*, 5 December 1983.
* Equity end of 1982; for US banks, equity of the leading bank of the group.

The policy decision

A bank may first think about the way and to what extent it would like to become involved in cross-border lending. This can be an active policy in the sense that a bank aims to obtain a certain percentage of its earnings from cross-border lending, or that it wants to limit its international exposure to a certain percentage of its balance sheet. It can also be a more passive policy in that a bank follows its domestic customers' international activity. Whatever the reasons for its international involvement, a bank should always make an assessment of its business potential in the international market, or at least fix a goal for its total international exposure. The goal is expressed in an amount that can be measured in relation to the total balance sheet, to the equity and/or to the funding potential, nationally or internationally, in order to estimate the opportunities and to calculate the risks involved. The bank must also bear in mind that cross-border lending often involves a different currency than the one in which it operates in its domestic activities.

Only after this assessment of principle about the international activity of a bank can the more detailed work of establishing country limits be made. It is advisable to formulate such a policy in writing.

Prudent banking means the spreading of risks and not only the following up of opportunities. The bank should, therefore, try to diversify its international business by analysing its potential in the different sectors of cross-border lending, bearing in mind its customers as well as geographical locations. This task is certainly time-consuming and needs a great deal of reflection. However, if it is not done in a serious way, the bank will find itself in the not-too-distant future with a country exposure portfolio of mixed blessings. In such an exercise it might also be worth while seeing if liabilities towards specific countries can be built up, rather than looking only at the asset potential. Liabilities of the Western banking system in this context are, for example, all the foreign currency reserves invested by central banks world-wide in the Western banking system. The trade pattern of a bank's own country can also give some hints regarding the potential for cross-border business with specific countries.

The risk assessment

At this stage, only country risk assessment should flow into the reflections, in order to guide a bank where it really wants to realise the potential of the market, and where a more restrictive approach seems advisable. The difficult choice between high risk/high return and low risk/low return will become evident. The bank might, therefore, establish a list of the countries where it has a potential to do business and incur cross-border exposure. In one column of the list a rough estimate of the potential would be made. The next column would give an indication about the assessment of the country risk, while the last column would show the country limit which would fix the maximum exposure the bank is willing to take towards these countries. This maximum should include direct and indirect risk because, especially for weaker countries, this is of significance. Such a list could be structured as in Table 9.2.

This is a very crude way, but sufficient for a first appreciation of the

Table 9.2. Structure of a country assessment list

Country	Potential	Risk score	Country limit
Netherlands	US$ 200m.	very low risk	US$200m.
Italy	US$ 800m.	low risk	US$600m.
India	US$ 500m.	medium risk	US$250m.
Mexico	US$1,000m.	moderately high risk	US$300m.
Zaïre	US$ 100m.	extremely high risk	—

situation. The risk scoring can obviously be much more refined, as explained under assessment of country risk. Furthermore, it is certainly questionable whether a direct relation between the potential, the risk score and the country limit can be established. For every country the relationship should be tailor-made in view of the bank's opportunities, goals and assessment of the risk involved.

The relation to equity

In fixing the size of the country limit, the bank must take into account not only the market potential of cross-border lending into that specific country and its assessment of the country risk involved, but also its capability to withstand the risk if it should ever materialise. The risk potential that emanates from cross-border lending must therefore be well diversified and be of a size that, even in a difficult situation, the solvency of the bank does not come into question. In this context the relation to the capital basis is a yardstick that can be used. A certain percentage of equity might become the upper limit for any country limit a bank establishes, because equity is the last cushion to absorb the shock of a loss. Banking legislation and supervisory authorities have established such limits in the past only for lending to specific customers but not to countries. Where they exist, they vary between 10 and 100 per cent of equity, showing that there is a wide variety of thinking on that subject.

Equity to total assets further varies considerably from country to country. The capabilities of the lender of last resort, who could overcome the liquidity problems of a banking system, also vary from country to country. It is therefore difficult to fix a general percentage of equity as the highest advisable country limit. However, each bank should attempt to do so, basing this primarily on its equity/assets relationship. Such a percentage can be differentiated for a group of countries, such as the LDCs and the OECD countries, or can encompass a wider group of countries. An exception to that percentage might be made at the very short end of the limit and for some very selected countries of especially high standing. Going above 50 per cent of equity for any country limit makes a bank very vulnerable in respect of country risk. This has to be seen not only in relation to its solvency; there is also a negative impact for its dealings with the borrowing country, since it will have too high a leverage. To fix the country limit in a lump sum only, is too crude a procedure, because this cannot take into account the different aspects of cross-border lending. The country limit has, therefore, to be structured – as will be seen later.

The country limit will be established in the currency the bank uses for its accounts. A West German bank would, therefore, use Deutschmarks, a Japanese bank the yen and a US bank the US dollar. The use of the currency of the bank's accounts and, therefore, of the bank's equity is the most adequate choice, because the final risk-taking capability of the bank is always in relation to equity. Changing currency relations do, as a result, affect the size of cross-border exposure within the country limit without any change in lending undertaken by the bank.

Necessity of reviews

The size of a country limit is variable rather than fixed. It will have to be adjusted to changing situations and circumstances. These can have their origin not only in a change in the quality of the country risk or in market opportunities, but also in a change in the policies of the bank. A change in utilisation can also be a factor, often the one in the forefront if the country limit is overdrawn.

It is a fact that most banks that engage in cross-border lending have already established their country limits using all kinds of different assumptions. Quite often the exposure was there even before a country limit was established, because that practice started on a wider scale only in the mid-1970s. It might, nevertheless, be worth while to carry out the exercise described above in reverse. Comparing the actual limits with the now estimated potential, also taking into account the risk scores and the capital basis, might introduce a new strategy for the marketing of a bank's international services. The analysis of potential discrepancies will lead to an improvement in monitoring country limits in the future.

Structure of the country limit

As we have direct and indirect country risk, the country limit could first be structured along these two major categories. Cross-border exposure comes further from all kinds of lending, so that the kind of lending could create another structure. Lending means not only different types of lending but also different kinds of maturities. In a further phase the maturity aspects could be dealt with, because we have seen their importance in the assessment of country risk. It would probably be too cumbersome and too difficult to monitor the country limit afterwards if it is structured in too many items, however. A certain simplified structure in rough categories seems to be appropriate.

Direct country risk

To begin, we might deal with lending under what we call direct country risk. Within the overall country limit a specific limit would have to be established for this risk. Such a limit for the total maximum exposure in direct country risk to a specific country would in a second step be divided into types of lending. A too fine division is again not recommended because it would be very difficult to monitor it effectively. A division into five broad separate categories would seem to be adequate.

Interbank transactions

Interbank lending would certainly have to be accounted for separately in the country limit and would constitute one category. It is normally the shortest type of lending into a country and as such is also easily defined. It would mean only clean advances to banks, with no connections to commercial transactions. The rates applied are principally those used in the interbank money market. A separate category for interbank lending also seems advisable in view of the special treatment interbank deposits have received in the recent reschedulings, particularly the Brazilian one.

Foreign exchange forward exposure

Another category would be the limit for foreign exchange forward exposure to a specific country. Such exposure can be calculated according to different systems; as a result, the size of the limit can vary substantially. Exactly matching contracts can, for example, be excluded because they create only settlement risks which can be neglected in connection with country risk assessment. Furthermore, as contracts can always be crossed out, it can also be argued that the limit for forward foreign exchange dealings need not cover the total exposure but only part of it. Obviously the country limits for interbank lending and forward foreign exchange dealings are of significance only for those countries with which such transactions are possible.

Other direct country exposure

The other three categories of the country limit would cover actual cross-border lending as it is normally understood. It is suggested, however, that the different types of lending be used as a way of determining not the three categories but the type of borrower. Country risk intensity is linked more to the status of the borrower than to the kind of lending. For all types of lending, country risk has the same meaning. Therefore, the categories could mean banks, excluding interbank and forward foreign exchange transactions, the private sector and the public sector. Such a division seems appropriate since each of the three categories has specific attributes in view of the assessment of country risk.

Banks

Lending to banks should be accounted for separately because banks normally operate in a special, regulated, economic environment. They are of major importance for each national economy and in a state of crisis have a special preferred status. They incorporate, therefore, a different credit risk than the rest of the economy of the country in question. Often they are also nationalised. However, no difference would be made between nationalised and private banks, because banks of a specific country normally not only operate along similar lines in their foreign operations but are often even similarly regulated.

Banks of the same country present the same country risk quality. The differentiation is obviously made by the size of credit exposure to the different banks in view of their credit standing. An exception could be made for the development banks, which do not carry out short-term commercial banking transactions. They could fall under the non-bank category. Banks, furthermore, maintain a two-way relationship with each other. They constitute not only an exposure to another bank but themselves take exposures on that bank. The possible exposures to banks are of a fairly short-term nature, because they are mostly in relation to trade. The exposure under this lending caption would exclude interbank transactions and foreign exchange forward transactions because they are accounted for separately. It would include all other exposures such as account relationship, documentary business, foreign exchange spot and other dealings, as well as lending under its different forms and maturities. The bank category would, therefore, be the third category within the structure of the country limit.

The private sector excluding banks

The private sector would be the next category of the country limit. It should be separated from the public sector so that one can clearly identify that part of cross-border lending where credit risk is as important as country risk, and where country risk quality can also be different. The difference in country risk quality stems from the experience that private creditors are often at a disadvantage in the attribution of foreign exchange when a country has liquidity problems. The risks that would be accounted for under this heading come from all the different types of lending that exist in cross-border lending. All types of maturities will also be a feature in this category. It is the most risky part of cross-border lending and should normally be undertaken only by banks that have a thorough understanding of the local environment and a well-established country risk assessment system.

The public sector excluding banks

In the fifth category would be grouped cross-border lending to the public sector of a specific country as well as to the government of that country. This category would further take into account not only lending to the public sector but also lending to private entities under a public-sector guarantee of the same country. Lending to the public sector is also called 'sovereign lending'. Much of that lending will have its origin in syndicated loans as well as capital market transactions. It is very often a medium- to long-term exposure.

Differing quality of country risk

For each country the potential of the five categories will have to be analysed, because in each country they offer different opportunities and often have a differing quality of risk. Banks might very well limit their cross-border lending to certain categories. Some of the categories enumerated are non-existent in specific countries because the transactions are not allowed or there are no borrowers in those categories. Nevertheless, it seems correct to use the same structure for all country limits in order to have a certain system for their establishment.

In this context it might be asked why the quality of country risk is different for the different categories. In principle this should not be the case when we look at country risk with the same maturities, because country risk is first of all in direct relation to a certain point in time. However, foreign exchange regulations often vary for the different sectors of the economy. Experience has shown that attribution of foreign exchange in a tight situation normally goes first to public bond issues and then to banks, then to government entities and only in the end to the private sector. Therefore, public bond issues and banks usually represent a better country risk than the other borrowers. On the other hand, one can establish in the private sector third-country guarantees which can reduce country risk – normally not possible in the public sector.

Indirect country risk

The second part of the country limit structure would be the exposures under indirect country risk. As already noted, this risk has its origin mainly in guarantee transactions from guarantors located in a country other than that of the guaranteed, and in lending to branches of banks which have their head office outside the country under discussion. Therefore, one could divide indirect country risk into two categories, namely indirect country risk exposure to banks and indirect country risk exposure to all other borrowers. This would again allow one to divide country risk according to its quality. A more refined division might be advisable under special circumstances. Indirect country exposure to banks can be quite substantial, since the banks of many countries use the big funding centres of the world to take up a large part of their foreign currency deposits, funding directly only their local assets.

The maturity profile

Having structured the country limit into the five categories of direct country risk and the two categories of indirect country risk, we should also establish a maturity profile for the different categories. Some of the categories present no special problems because they are only short-term exposures. But for all the other categories maturity profiles would have to be established. For these it is certainly accepted that one must first clearly identify the short-term, i.e. the exposure up to one year, and the rest. The short-term might even be divided into up to six months and over six months. Regarding the structure of the rest there are basically three options: either lump them all together, divide them up on a yearly basis, or try to make some sensible groupings into medium-term and long-term. Each bank has to find the best structure for exposures over a year according to its own operations. Furthermore, the reporting system to the banking supervisory authorities might influence the division or give some guidance for it. A reasonable division could be a breakdown into 2–3 years, 4–5 years, 6–10 years and more than 10 years, if the lending portfolio is substantial in terms of quantity and diversified in terms of customers and maturity. A

Table 9.3. Structure for a country limit

Country: X	Total	Up to 1 yr	2–3 yrs	4–5 yrs	6–10 yrs	Over 10 yrs
Direct country risk						
Interbank lending	150	150	—	—	—	—
Forward foreign exchange exposure	20	20	—	—	—	—
Banks	150	120	15	15	—	—
Private sector	380	100	70	70	70	70
Public sector	100	10	—	—	50	40
Total direct country risk	800	400	85	85	120	110
Indirect country risk						
Banks	40	40	—	—	—	—
Others	10	10	—	—	—	—
Total indirect country risk	50	50	—	—	—	—
Total country limit	850	450	85	85	120	110

Total limit US$850 million — Maturities

possible structure for a country limit could, therefore, resemble the one shown in Table 9.3.

A structure of the country limit as proposed postulates a breakup of the total sum into about 20 different items. This already involves a fairly substantial exercise in reaching the optimum result because there is no standard breakup. Each category and maturity has to be established based on a management decision. Further refinements in the country limit structure through additional categories are obviously possible, but substantially increase the task of forecasting because each part has to be handled separately. It should always be borne in mind that the country limit structure is the basis not only for monitoring a country exposure but also for the marketing policy of the bank in that specific country. It should, therefore, be understandable and realisable.

The structure of a country limit is thus not only the outflow of a technical solution but also the expression of the policy adopted by the bank towards that country.

Responsibilities for fixing the country limit

Establishing and structuring a country limit always involves the assessment of country risk as well as an estimate of the market potential of the specific country for cross-border transactions. It can, therefore, also be part of a marketing plan. Country experts and marketing specialists will have the necessary depth of knowledge to arrive at a good estimate of potential. For larger banks, which often have these specialists, the establishment of potential is of more importance than for smaller and medium-sized banks, because their potential will be a significant part of the total market potential for cross-border exposure into that country. The limit-setting will then be made by looking for a specific market share goal in view of the country risk involved and its assessment.

The medium-sized and smaller banks normally do not have a specific market share in mind; they look mainly for an interesting return on their cross-border lending by taking into account their assessment of the country risk and the needs of their customers. For them it is, therefore, the relationship risk score/country limit/customer need that is of major importance, while larger banks are in addition sensitive to the market share question. They will all look for a good diversification within the number of different country risks.

Fixing the size of country limits is, nevertheless, a highly important decision for every bank, because it involves not only the decision about risk-taking of a complex character, but normally also quite substantial amounts. It is, therefore, the task of top managements to make those decisions; it would be imprudent to leave them to the lower echelons of the management hierarchy. Proposals for the limits will have to be prepared by regional managements if such an organisational structure is used. The approval and, therefore, the fixing of the limit should be done in the upper echelons of management in a way similar to that in which credit lines are approved in the bank. Some banks use a committee system, whereas others leave it up to an individual or a group of individuals to approve such limits. Some banks even have special country risk committees. Different ways are certainly suitable; the important thing is that a clear procedure exists for approving and fixing country limits similar to the one banks have used for credit lines for many years. Most supervisory authorities today, therefore, inquire not only about the size of country limits and respective exposures, but also about the procedures for fixing them.

10

Monitoring country exposure

General aspects

The establishment of a country limit is the basis for limiting the total risk of cross-border transactions into a specific country. While the country limit is fixed and reviewed from time to time, the exposure will vary on a daily basis. The monitoring of country exposure should enable the bank to make in time the necessary decisions to seize new opportunities and, therefore, expand its exposure – but should also enable it to foresee in time a deteriorating situation and, therefore, to contain or reduce its exposure. In order to do so, the monitoring should encompass the risk assessment, exposure management and country limit review, as well as making provision for country risk if necessary. The task of monitoring should be conferred on specialists within the bank. These specialists should not be the same that approve the limits. There are different organisational approaches to locate these specialists within a bank's structuring. In a smaller bank it will be the international division; in larger establishments we find a regional management or country specialist organisation to look after the monitoring of country exposures. The essential thing is that the task of monitoring country risk is clearly assigned within the bank, just as the monitoring of credit risk has always been.

In addition, monitoring the country limit can be valid only when it is on a consolidated basis for the bank in question. It must take into account not only all the branches but also all the subsidiaries of the banking group.

Choice of a system for the assessment of country risk

In monitoring country exposure, the monitoring of the quality of the country risk is one of the major objectives. In monitoring a credit risk the balance sheet, as well as the profit and loss statement of the debtor, are reviewed periodically to evaluate the quality of the risk. In monitoring country risk we must evaluate its quality by assessing it at regular intervals. The system chosen should, therefore, make this possible.

In Part Two the different methods currently used to assess country risk were explained. To obtain the necessary quality in assessing country risk at regular intervals a bank must therefore choose its own system.

It is obviously important what system a bank chooses; even more important is that the bank adheres to the same system over a certain period of time, in order to reach consistency of assessment and to find out if the chosen system is relevant for the operation it runs. The use of a readily available scoring system, such as those outlined in Chapter 8, is often more advisable than trying to construct a tailor-made system, which is certainly at least as costly as the readily available one and quite often not much more accurate. A larger institution will, however, normally work out its own system, in order to adapt it to the goals it wants to achieve in cross-border exposure monitoring.

Foreseeing a change in the quality of country risk

The system it chooses should enable the institution to realise the changing quality of the country risk. More than looking at the past, the chosen system should focus on the possible developments of the future. In this context, the prompt recognition of a change in risk quality and correct forecasting of a forthcoming rescheduling mean a lot, since they help to contain the exposure and to avoid in time new commitments of funds: rescheduling usually leads to forced new commitments.

In view of the constantly changing situation in country risk quality, the system chosen should allow for the assessment of country risk at least at six-month intervals. Political and transfer risk assessment must be organised and based on up-to-date information that is available at regular intervals. Country limits of the countries that are considered medium or higher risks need to be reviewed at even shorter intervals, in order not only to stop new commitments but also to take advantage of possible new opportunities when the risks are decreasing. A change in the quality of the country risk can lead, for example, to a worsening of the situation in the private sector while having no impact on the public sector. It can also mean that the opportunity for medium-term lending is improving due to newly found natural resources, while the short-term outlook is still bleak. In such a situation it is a possible change in the structure of the country limit that should be evaluated, without changing the overall limit. The assessment system chosen should, therefore, help a bank in making this kind of decision, not focusing only on changes in the total size of the limit. The chosen system should allow a bank to change the country limit or the structure of the limit at regular intervals in view of actual developments which are likely to affect the country risk.

It is not the most sophisticated assessment system which will lead to successful country exposure management, but a system that produces continuously the correct fever curve of the country in question. It should convey warning signals such as wildly inflated military expenditure, unrealistic exchange rates, massive short-term borrowing or discrimination among foreign investments. The matrix system gives the bank a good and relatively easy method of following up the development of country risk at meaningful intervals. Changing from one square to another would immediately alert management about a change in the quality of country risk and enable it to undertake the necessary action.

Monitoring the country exposure

While review of the country limit through the chosen system of country risk assessment gives the bank the necessary indications regarding its overall policy towards a country, the daily monitoring of country exposure helps in fine tuning cross-border exposure. Through the monitoring of the exposure, the bank will at regular intervals be in a position to account for its exposure to a specific country in the same categories as are identified in its structure of the country limit. Country exposure tends to be closer to country limits in countries with higher risk than in countries with lower risk. The monitoring of the exposure, therefore, has a double purpose. In the low risk countries the monitoring can help to identify constantly the sectors where the bank is still looking for business opportunities. It is, therefore, an instrument in marketing the bank's services towards a specific country. On the other hand, monitoring the country exposure in high risk countries will help to contain the exposure, or shift it in the direction the bank desires.

Through the monitoring the bank will also be able to maintain the same diversification of risk as it planned when it established the country limits and their structures. A bank must be especially careful not to find itself at the end of the day with fully used limits in countries with a difficult situation and unused country limits in the so-called 'premium countries'. Furthermore, it should not suddenly find that the major part of its commitments are in the long maturities of the country limit. Such developments would point to an inefficient monitoring system.

The bank should also know not only all the actual exposures but also all its commitments to a specific country, in order to evaluate its maximum possible total exposure. Such commitments can be confirmed but not fully used credit lines, stand-by lines, confirmed letters of credit, guarantees and credit offers.

The ability to monitor correctly the country exposure of a large internationally operating bank needs a substantial infrastructure. The accounting system used for normal balance sheet purposes is certainly not sufficient, since the country risk structure follows other principles.

A specific organisation as well as procedures must therefore be set up to control and monitor the bank's country risk exposure, real and potential, within the authorised country limits. Special computer programs will be needed to assure that country exposure data are readily available to the bank. Such total exposure data should always be available on a group level, i.e. on a consolidated basis, in order to be meaningful. The necessary effort to obtain the respective data is certainly worth while undertaking and is now even prescribed by many banking supervisory authorities world-wide. This is usually the task of the international division's country desk and respective country officers. In many banks these country desks are located at headquarters. However, some large internationally operating banks have their country desks on the Continent or in the hemisphere where the country is located. Both approaches have their advantages and disadvantages, and the choice will depend on the size of the international organisation and on the concept of marketing the international services of the bank. Furthermore, banks do delegate specific parts of the country limits, such as the interbank country lending limit, to their treasury operations in order to obtain the needed efficiency in the decision-making process.

Through internal reporting channels, each proposal for taking up a specific country risk should come to the person responsible for the monitoring of that risk – in most cases the respective country desk. There it must be evaluated, in order to find out if it can be fitted into the country's limit structure and current policy towards that country. If the country risk and, therefore, the transaction is then approved, the country desk must make sure that the commitment is accounted for as a potential exposure. From that moment onwards the transaction must be monitored by the country desk. At each moment the country desk should be in a position to know in what stage of development the proposed transaction is. How are the two parts of the transaction, namely the commitment and the actual exposure, moving along? Are the details regarding amounts and maturities always known? This can be fairly easy for a simple transaction such as interbank lending, but can be quite complicated, for example, for a seven-year standby credit with multicurrency clauses that is only partly drawn down.

The organisation of the bank must ensure that every proposed transaction involving a country risk obtains correct country risk clearance and is then monitored as explained above. The country officer, for his part, must monitor his country exposure in such a way that it reflects the marketing policy of the bank for that country, is well in line with the current risk assessment of the country, and fits into the structure of the authorised country limit. Only then can an optimum between risk and reward be obtained in cross-border lending. In this context, the real time availability of each country exposure is an aimed-for state of organisation achievement for every bank.

The change of country risk quality

If an assessment system with periodical reviews is institutionalised, it should give the first indications of a change in the risk quality of a specific country. It would be up to the decision level at the bank to fix at which scoring points, range of scoring points or change of scoring points a review of business and marketing policies should be made. The review obviously does not automatically lead to a change of policy, but obliges the different departments concerned with that particular cross-border exposure to reassess the bank's policy towards the country. It is certainly helpful in this context if the bank's management fixes broad policies of behaviour for specific ranges of ratings. This could mean that only certain types of cross-border exposures are undertaken at a given score and that maturity structures are related to a specific rating. Through such a system the bank obtains a coherent policy between its rating of the assessment system and its exposure.

A deteriorating situation

If the situation is deteriorating, the bank has several possibilities to contain or reduce its risk. In the first place, it will fix its exposure at the current amount outstanding regardless of the authorised country limit. Then an adjustment of the country limit to the new situation will have to be made. The analysis and comparison between the new country limit and the existing exposure will make clear what kind of action should be undertaken.

The adjustment process will always be a difficult procedure. It will be especially difficult if the deterioration is already known to the whole banking community. If it is, however, spotted well in advance, the adjustment process can be done in a very orderly way. Checking out the obtained change in the rating through a visit on the spot is always advisable if it has not already been done. Such a visit will give the necessary insight into what kind of action by the lender will be possible and what kind of action would need further analysis.

There are several actions that can be undertaken. They are similar to those taken when a domestic creditor faces increasing difficulties. As in such a case, at each stage of risk change other measures will be needed. The following measures are, therefore, to be viewed in this context.

Basic steps

Unconfirmed and unused credit lines can always be suspended. Confirmed credit lines, on the other hand, can be reduced or cancelled only on the respective possible dates. For new business that will have to be undertaken, the maturity structure must be watched very carefully. It is generally

111

assumed that exposures with shorter maturities are easier to collect than those with longer maturities. This is certainly true as long as the situation is not yet too alarming. In financing international trade, the importance of the goods exported to the economy in question, such as energy or food, can also give some clues to what kind of commitment should be undertaken. Margins and fees will have to be reviewed when the quality of risk is changing, in order to take into account the riskiness of the business. However, the markets so far do not seem to honour that fact well enough, because margins are still guided more by the availability of a service and by the competitiveness of the market than by the risk involved in such transactions.

Risk sharing

The possibility of sharing the risk with a partner also reduces the overall risk. Such sharing can be done between banks on a disclosed or non-disclosed basis for the borrower. The same kind of thought lies behind the syndication of risks. In this case the risk is shared among several partners, with one bank functioning as lead bank. Syndication involves quite a substantial amount of administrative work and is therefore meaningful only if large amounts are involved.

Risk sharing can be undertaken only when the quality of the country risk is still acceptable to a large segment of the market participants.

Third-country guarantees

To reduce country risk in one country, it might also be possible to obtain a guarantee from a third country with a better country risk rating. Such a procedure is often used when lending to a subsidiary of a borrower who is located in a very low risk country. It is obviously advisable to envisage such a guarantee at a very early stage of the basic transaction, because it might be difficult to obtain it when the downgrading of the rating is already common knowledge.

Counter-claims

Building up a counter-claim is another way of reducing the risk. Such counter-claims can be deposits emanating from the country in question, which can then be used to reduce one's own risk. They must, however, be pledged. In this connection one remembers the pledging of part of the gold reserve by Portugal to obtain foreign credits. Counter-claims must in addition be acceptable under the legislation of the country involved.

Selling of assets

A further possibility to manage country risk change is selling assets of the country in question. Such a transaction is usually highly sensitive since it needs the consent of the borrower. Normally it is done with a certain discount in order to make the transaction attractive to the buyer. In connection with the rescheduled assets of some of the LDCs, efforts have been made to create a market for them. So far it has boiled down mainly to the swapping of assets of different countries, each valued separately, and not the straight selling of assets at a special discount. It must be added that for the time being these transactions have been relatively rare and of a fairly marginal size.

An improving situation

If the assessment of a specific country risk shows an improvement, the action to be undertaken moves in the opposite sense. It is equally important to recognise such a development in time in order not to miss potential opportunities. To be a latecomer involves no losses, but does mean reduced earnings due to the more competitive environment that develops in such a situation.

A change in country risk quality should always demand action by those responsible for the country involved. The change is in direct correlation to the assessment of the risk. If the risk has reached a certain level, the question of provisions should be dealt with.

Provisions for country risk

As long as cross-border lending was not associated with the term 'country risk', special provisions for country risk were unknown, because no specific risk was conceived of beyond credit risk. As country risk is today clearly identified as a specific risk in cross-border lending, the question of provisions has become a real issue. Provisions for country risk can be made on an allocated basis or in the form of general reserves. Allocated provisions are made when the risk has become so apparent that its materialisation is only a matter of time. The provisions made are then balanced off against the necessary write-off when the effective loss is incurred. In the case of country risks, effective losses have so far been incurred only when debt was repudiated, fortunately a very rare occasion to date.

Provisions can further be made on a pre-tax or after-tax basis. In the first case taxable income is reduced and, therefore, the tax authorities are very interested in the issue. In both cases the shareholders also have an interest in the way the provisions are made since their income, the dividends, are paid out from the after-tax result. The dogma that countries cannot go bankrupt made both tax authorities and shareholders resist general provisions for country risk in many countries for many years. In addition, the supervisory authorities in several countries went along with that reasoning for quite some time. The events of the past few years have, however, changed that attitude. In this context the decision by the IV Senate of the

Financial Tribunal of Hesse (West Germany) in August 1982 was significant, as it accepted a 50 per cent provision before tax on loans to Poland at the request of a foreign bank in Frankfurt. Furthermore, the bold stroke by John S. Reed, Chairman of Citicorp, in reserving three billion US dollars against country risk exposure towards Third World Countries in May 1987 has made it finally clear to all bankers that prudent banking also means setting up provisions or reserves for country risk, as has been common practice for credit risk all along.

The systems used vary from country to country. The general trend is that for countries in severe difficulties, often identified by the supervisory authorities, specific reserves must be set up. These allocated transfer risk reserves are normally fixed at least at 10 per cent of the principal amount of the asset and must be provided for on a yearly basis as long as the asset is in the same category of risk. They are set up before tax. General reserves against country risk are not yet a common feature, but have been adopted in several European countries and are now also adopted by major US banks. As the general reserve is made against the total of the loan portfolio, it is also a certain percentage of total country risk exposure. It cannot always be made before tax.

Prudent monitoring of country exposure must consider the aspects of provisions for country risk. The management of the bank must be aware of this. While the supervisory authorities might give guidance on provisions or even require certain provisions, it is still the task of the country officer and country desk to work out a provision scheme, country by country, in view of the risks involved. Furthermore, the provision scheme could allocate certain reserves against groups of specific countries, like insurance against a specific type of risk, or work out a general provision for the total of all country risk exposures. For most countries no provision is probably needed. The country risk assessment scheme will be a helpful guide in working out provisions. Such an exercise is even more important for banks that receive no guidance from their supervisory authorities.

11

Refinancing aspects

The currency problem

The different aspects of the risks involved in the relation between assets and liabilities in a bank's balance sheet are well known. To deal with several of these aspects, the golden rules of banking have been established. One of these principles is that transformation of maturities and currencies between the assets and liabilities side of the balance sheet should stay in certain relation. Specific types of assets should correspond to certain types of liabilities. Depending on the activity of the bank, there are different ways to obtain a defensible balance. However, there are special situations in view of a bank's position.

The two extreme situations are the bank that has no natural refinancing sources but is striving actively for assets, such as many consortium banks, and the bank that has a large amount of funds from the public but difficulties in building a broad portfolio of assets, such as many savings banks. Depending on its specific situation, which is normally between those two extremes, one can qualify the refinancing situation for a bank as more or less comfortable.

Assets that involve not only a credit risk but also a country risk are, as noted earlier, mainly denominated in one of the currencies used in international financing and must, therefore, be refinanced in the same currency. Of all these currencies the US dollar plays by far the most dominant role. Banks that engage actively in cross-border lending will thus have a substantial US dollar loan portfolio to refinance. This is certainly a different task for a US dollar-based bank than for all the other banks. *Mutatis mutandis* the situation is, however, similar for US banks that participate in a Deutschmark loan. Most of the internationally syndicated loans contain multicurrency clauses which, in view of interest and parity expectations, can lead to changing patterns of borrowed currencies. Therefore, nearly every bank engaged in cross-border lending must consider refinancing in a foreign currency to a certain extent.

Banks with a larger foreign currency asset portfolio can face major problems in their refinancing. In a liquidity crisis they have no lender of last resort for these foreign currency assets. The central banks function only in the domestic market as lender of last resort. For foreign currencies, central banks have only a limited potential to assist their banks. It might be argued that the swap market will always function and take care of such a situation, or that the non-availability clause of the syndicated loan agreement can be invoked and, therefore, another currency be offered. Under normal circumstances both these arguments have their appeal. However, we cannot disregard the problems inherent in this situation, especially when we assume a certain turmoil in international financial markets.

Most banks have no natural source for refinancing their foreign currency assets in that same currency. Instead they must rely heavily on the interbank money market. In a drying up of that market and/or in a tiering of the market, banks that depend heavily on it can face either liquidity problems or at least higher costs for their funding. Developments in that direction have always been observed in crisis situations and in their aftermath. The Herstatt collapse, the Latin American debt crisis, the Ambrosiano scandal and the Schroder Münchmeyer Hengst affair all had their complications for specific segments of banks, giving them a tough time for the refinancing of their foreign currency assets. Fortunately the international banking community assisted by the different central banks has so far had the strength to survive such circumstances and, therefore, to make the tense situation fairly short-lived. It is, nevertheless, important that banks with foreign currency assets look for ways and means to obtain a stable foreign currency refinancing basis. They should avoid relying simply on the interbank market for foreign currencies, and find other sources of refinancing for at least a part of their international lending portfolio.

Maturity transformation

Maturity transformation has always been an important task for bankers in bringing together the funds obtained from the market and the funds lent to the market. In addition, we find maturity transformations on the same side of the balance sheet due to technical reasons. Savings accounts can normally be withdrawn at short notice but are, in view of their great diversity in amounts and their great number, considered a medium-term refinancing instrument. Similar situations can be found on the assets side of the balance sheet. In domestic lending the short-term overdraft facility is often in fact a medium-term lending proposition. But the essential maturity transformation is made between the asset and liability sides of a bank's balance sheet.

Cross-border lending is a market segment that uses maturity transformation in the traditional sense extensively between assets and liabilities, especially in medium-term lending. In order to alleviate the refinancing problem of medium-term lending, the syndicated loan market has been created. While the loan may extend for seven years, the actual interest period is fixed for only six months; the refinancing needed is a corresponding six-month instrument – which has usually been the six-month inter-bank deposit. The interest mismatch, which is one of the dangers in maturity transformation, can be eliminated through such an instrument. Unsolved, however, is the availability problem for the lender or the disposability of funds for the borrower at each rollover date. In time of crisis, which can also mean only a substantial uncertainty about the development of interest rates, a contraction of the interbank market to even shorter maturities than the normal six months can be observed. Therefore, banks are obliged to incur an interest risk and to lend at terms such as six months, while having to refinance themselves in the interbank market at shorter maturities such as one to three months. A development of this kind shows its effects mainly on the profit and loss statement of the bank concerned and does not create a liquidity problem.

The interest differentials between the one-month and three-months' interest level and the six-months' level are, in relatively stable market situations, positive for the short end. The bank can, therefore, profit from this situation and borrow even shorter than it lends. This is especially helpful when margins on medium credit are tight. It is, however, a fairly risky game since the situation can change suddenly.

Availability of funds

As on each rollover date funds must be available, banks try to find refinancing sources that cope with these requirements. For most banks concerned it means assuring themselves of an ample supply of time deposits with six-month maturities. It is normally not necessary for a bank to obtain medium- and long-term fixed-rate funds. The supply of six-month funds is currently assured through the interbank market for banks that have a good credit standing and present an acceptable country risk. In the interbank market credit lines are in general not confirmed and availability is, therefore, tied to market conditions. A contraction of the interbank market due to the shifting of the liquid assets placed there into other assets has, therefore, an immediate impact on the ease of availability of funds. Such a shift can, for example, occur in an economic upswing, when corporate loan demand suddenly picks up. Investors can withdraw from the short-term market when the interest level in the long-term market becomes attractive.

In order to cope with the problem of unstable availability in the interbank market, banks with large portfolios of cross-border assets must find stable sources of supply. This has always been the goal of conservative bankers. Several refinancing instruments are available to deal with this situation.

Refinancing instruments

Stand-by credit

Stand-by credits with a large US dollar-based city bank are a means for smaller banks to cover their risk emanating from the refinancing aspects of their cross-border exposures. Stand-by credits are a fairly simple instrument. The borrowing bank usually has to pay only a front-end fee and a commitment fee over the running period of the stand-by credit. As the refinancing basis of the large US banks has become in the recent past not only more expensive but also more volatile due to developments in domestic markets (such as higher interest awareness of the depositor and better communication techniques), the availability of stand-by credits is also undergoing change. Banks are no longer as willing as they were to grant them. Through a stand-by credit the US bank becomes effectively the lender of last resort for the amount of the stand-by for the non-US bank to refinance its US dollar loan and asset portfolio. A similar credit construction can obviously be made for other currencies. Therefore, Deutschmark exposures can be refinanced through a stand-by with some of the large Deutschmark-based banks.

Supervisory authorities, especially the Bank of England, have resorted to stand-by agreements and asked for them in order to assure the adequate and correct refinancing of London banking subsidiaries as well as London consortium banks. In the latter case the shareholding banks must arrange the stand-by agreement.

The floating rate note issues

Since the interbank market is no longer regarded as an endlessly renewable source of available funds, and since stand-by credits are difficult to arrange for larger internationally operating banks, new ways had to be found to obtain medium-term funds to refinance the loan portfolio, in particular the assets involved in the different rescheduling exercises. The floating rate note (FRN) issue has been the most popular way to obtain such funds. It is an issue whereby the borrowing bank obtains a certain amount, usually in tens of millions of US dollars, for a period of several years. The time period up to which funds can be obtained varies substantially from bank to bank, depending mainly on its standing in the international banking community. The average is, however, between seven and 12 years.

The interest rate is normally fixed for a six-month period on the basis of LIBOR with a margin. This margin is again influenced by the standing of the bank as well as by prevailing market conditions. Owing to the high competitiveness of the FRN market, margins have decreased since mid-1983; at the beginning of 1984 they were normally below $\frac{1}{8}$ per cent and have since become even finer. The arranging syndicate in addition receives front-end fees for the placing and selling of the issue. LIBOR is fixed by a number of so-called reference banks periodically, on the date of the beginning of the new interest period for the issue in question. In the first three months of 1984 the FRN issues shown in Table 11.1 were taken up by banks in the Euromarket.

Table 11.1. Floating rate note issues, January–March 1984

Bank	US$ million	Maturity	%
The Bank of New York	75,000	84–96	100
Crédit Lyonnais	250,000	84–96	100
Creditanstalt-Bankverein	125,000	84–94	100
Die Erste Oesterreichische Sparkasse	50,000	84–92	100
Fuji International Finance Corp.	200,000	84–96	100
Morgan Grenfell Investment	50,000	84–94	100
National Bank of Canada	50,000	84–91	100
Standard Chartered Finance	200,000	84–94	100
Banque Nationale de Paris	400,000	84–95	100
Commerzbank International Finance	100,000	84–89	100
Crédit Commercial de Paris	250,000	84–96	100
Creditanstalt-Bankverein	150,000	84–96	100
Dresdner Finance	350,000	84–89	100
Grindlays Eurofinance	100,000	84–94	100
Hill Samuel Finance	30,000	84–96	100
Kansallis-Osake-Pankki	100,000	84–92	100
Sanwa International Finance	150,000	84–92	100
Sumitomo Trust Finance (Hong Kong)	100,000	84–94	100
Union Bank of Norway	50,000	84–99	100
Arab Banking Corp.	100,000	84–96	100
Arbuthnot Latham Finance	30,000	84–92	100
Banque Indosuez	150,000	84–99	100
Barclays Overseas Investment	350,000	84–94	100
BBL International	100,000	84–99	100
BfG Finance Co.	100,000	84–96	100
Midland International Finance Service	200,000	84–99	100
Okobank	50,000	84–92	100
Société Générale	250,000	84–94	100

Source: Institutional Investor.

Banks have been the major borrower in the FRN market and have thus obtained substantial amounts of medium- and long-term funds to refinance their rescheduled assets, among others.

A variation of interest computation every six months is the adjustment of the rate every month while pay-out of the interest is maintained at a three-months' or six-months' rhythm.

From the investors' point of view, the FRN is especially interesting in times of higher interest rate expectations. FRN issues are also of interest in times of highly volatile interest rates. It must further be noted that the FRN theoretically eliminates the potential of a price risk if the bond is kept until the end of an interest period. Market forces so far have not always performed in such a way, but the price risk still remains fairly limited with the exception of the perpetual floater. On the other hand, the FRN rarely has a potential for a substantial price appreciation.

Buyers of the FRN have to a large extent been central banks and commercial banks, which took them onto their books instead of the more risky and less liquid syndicated loan assets. The commercial banks, in buying the notes, may create a refinancing risk for themselves. It would, therefore, be more advisable for the Euromarket participants to place the FRN issues of banks with institutional investors outside the banking community. With such a procedure the FRN issues do not use interbank liquidity for financing, but are financed on the basis of the financial strength of the institutional investors. Banks that depend heavily on the interbank market for their refinancing should especially not buy FRN issues of other banks because they could provoke a chain reaction in time of crisis and substantially aggravate interbank market liquidity. They would probably no longer be in a position to refinance themselves and, therefore, finance the FRN assets.

Another critical element is currently the limited secondary market for FRN issues. The London issuing and trading houses must create a much larger market for these notes in order to add the necessary depth to the market. Only then does this instrument live up to its concept, namely by providing the bank with the necessary medium-term funds and giving the investor a really negotiable instrument which he can sell at any time.

The banks issuing FRN still do some maturity transformation because it is unlikely for them that the issuing dates of the FRN will match the rollover dates of their syndicated loan assets. To cover these risks the bank can today revert to the Financial Futures markets. The FRN issue is a more expensive source of refinancing than the interbank market but gives a secure supply of medium- and long-term funds.

Certificate of Deposit Issuance Facility

The Certificate of Deposit Issuance Facility is another instrument that gives the borrowing bank access to medium-term funds through a short-term money market instrument. Certificates of Deposit (CDs) are basically short-term deposits with a bank that issues the CD for the amount received. The CD is negotiable; it can be bought and sold in an active and broad secondary market. Buyers of CDs are a wide range of investors that include corporations, institutional investors, wealthy private individuals, and central and commercial banks. The issuing houses that arrange a Certificate of Deposit Issuance Facility undertake together with the other members of the syndicate to purchase a maximum given amount of CDs from the borrowing bank at any time during the life of the facility. The members of the syndicate receive a commitment fee for selling the CDs as well as an issuance fee when the certificates are sold.

The advantage for the borrowing bank is that during the life of the facility it always has access to short-term funds which can automatically be rolled over at maturity date. The participants in the facility must, on the other hand, make sure that they can always place the CDs in the market. It is questionable whether in a difficult interbank market this will be an easy undertaking. Issuing houses with a large placing power are, therefore, the best ones to undertake this kind of capital market transaction. The CD Issuance Facility has, due to this placement aspect and to its pricing structure, lost some of its appeal lately.

Variations of this facility are the Note Issuance Facility (NIF) and the Revolving Underwriting Facility (RUF). Through these facilities a major US issuing house undertakes to place continuously, over the life of the facility, the CDs of the borrowing bank. The participating banks in the RUF, for their part, undertake to underwrite all those CDs that the issuing house cannot place at any time during the life of the facility. The participating banks receive a commitment fee for their service. The borrowing bank again has access to funds over a substantial period of time to refinance its medium-term assets.

The borrowing banks can obtain through a Certificate of Deposit Issuance Facility the exactly matching funds for their assets, for a certain price. The underwriting and participating banks obtain a fairly interesting commitment fee, but must at all times be in a position to sell the underwritten commitments. Therefore, this facility has never reached the popularity of the FRN issues, where the underwritten amount is sold when the issue is launched.

Swap arrangements

While swap arrangements in foreign exchange markets have been known for many years, they are a relatively new instrument in capital markets. A swap in the foreign exchange market means that a bank sells to another bank, for example, US dollars against Swiss francs, and undertakes to buy back these US dollars at a future date against delivery of the Swiss francs. It is, therefore, an exchange transaction. In the Eurocapital markets the swap of liabilities has become an important kind of transaction. Of the different liabilities it is the interest liabilities that have become the basis of most of the swap arrangements. The interest swap is the exchange of interest liabilities that are differently calculated. A variable interest liability calculated on LIBOR or prime basis is swapped against a fixed-rate interest liability. The partners in the swap arrangement do not exchange the capital but limit their agreement to the corresponding take-over of interest liabilities during the lifetime of the underlying transaction.

A more complicated swap arrangement is one where the currencies are also swapped because one capital market transaction is made in a non-US-dollar currency and the other in US dollars. In such a case not only has the interest swap to be made but also a currency swap. It then involves both interest and principle. Each partner takes over the liabilities of the other, while the currency involved is not hedged. Very often a prime bank acts as middleman and, therefore, guarantees the obligation to each partner. The interest liabilities can be either fixed-rate for both currencies, or on the one side fixed-rate and on the other side variable. In the latter situation this transaction is called a cross-currency interest rate swap.

In order to make swap operations interesting for both partners, they must have a different credit standing. While one partner is normally a first-class address with highly visible market acceptance, the other address is often less well known. Typically, this involves in the Eurobond market a fixed-rate bond of a prime bank which then swaps its interest obligation with a floating-rate obligation of another borrower, very often a medium-sized US company of good standing. From the transaction the fixed-rate borrowing bank obtains floating-rate US dollars at a substantially lower cost than LIBOR, while the floating-rate borrowing US company obtains fixed-rate US dollars at conditions which it could otherwise never obtain.

The World Bank was involved in many cross-currency interest rate swaps where Swiss francs and US dollars were involved. Due to its frequent use of the Swiss capital market, the World Bank had to pay slightly higher rates than other prime borrowers. In order to overcome this obstacle to obtaining fixed-rate long-term Swiss francs at an advantageous rate, it borrowed in the US dollar floating-rate long-term market, where it has a triple A rating, and swapped these US dollars with a commercial bank that needed the floating-rate US-dollars. This commercial bank then provided the World Bank with the fixed-rate long-term Swiss francs which it took up in the market at a fine rate with the same end-maturity date; thus both banks obtained the desired currencies at satisfactory rates.

Swap transactions are possible not only with new issues; they can also be made on one side with a new one while the other side is already running. Swap transactions have in recent times become much more competitive and numerous than in the past. They involve many corporate as well as sovereign borrowers beside the banks. They are an interesting way for banks to optimise their funding basis. Through swaps banks can often obtain their funds at a better rate than if they took up an FRN issue or a CD facility. These transactions are arranged by the well-known issuing houses as well as by major internationally operating banks with a broad customer basis.

12

The role of banking supervision

General aspects

The supervision of banks in connection with country risk has become a concern for all banking supervisory authorities since the beginning of the big boom in international lending in the 1970s. Through the Committee on Banking Regulations and Supervisory Practices, created in 1974 in the aftermath of the Herstatt crisis by the Governors of the Group of Ten, banking supervisory bodies today co-ordinate their efforts in respect to country risk. The Committee on Banking Regulations and Supervisory Practices has been headed since its creation by Peter Cooke, Head of Banking Supervision at the Bank of England, and is, therefore, currently known as the Cooke Committee. It convenes regularly in Basle at the headquarters of the Bank for International Settlements. With respect to country risk supervision, the question of jurisdiction must first be answered in order to know which banking supervisory body is responsible for what bank or branch of a bank. Through the so-called Basle Concordat of 1975, which was endorsed by the Board of Directors of the Bank for International Settlements, it was accepted that in principle the responsibility for supervision of a bank and its branch network lies with the supervisory authority responsible for the head office of the bank. In 1982 the Cooke Committee gave some recommendations with respect to country risk to the supervisory authorities of the member countries of the Group of Ten. These guidelines have also been adopted by other supervisory authorities.

The guidelines confirm that it is basically the responsibility of the management of the banks to decide what kind of cross-border transactions they would like to undertake. This is analogous to the restraint of banking supervisory authorities with respect to domestic lending, where there is no interference in the choice of borrower that a bank can lend to. Banking supervisory authorities are, however, asked to be involved in cross-border lending and to review the country risks undertaken by the banking system of their respective countries. These authorities should further ensure that the banks of their countries use adequate methods to assess and monitor their country risks.

In the first place, it is important that supervisory authorities know that each bank involved in cross-border transactions uses a specific system to assess its country risk. The bank should be in a position to use the chosen system competently and make the necessary means available so that the system functions. The banking supervisory authorities should themselves be in a position to evaluate the assessment system chosen by the bank, in order to guide it if it feels that the system needs to be improved. Banking supervisory bodies are advised by the Cooke Committee not to create country risk assessment schemes for their banks, but to leave this task to the banks themselves.

A second aspect with which the banking supervisory authorities have to deal is the monitoring of country risk. Supervision of monitoring means that the supervisory authorities must make sure that the banks have a system that enables them to compile their country exposure at regular intervals. This compilation of country exposure should be detailed enough so that the supervisory bodies can not only assess the risk but also obtain a view of its diversification. In addition, the authorities must ensure that the banks use their assessment system for country risk to continuously monitor their exposure. In this context the establishment of country limits will have to be controlled. The supervisory authority must also assure itself that the country limit system used by the banks is functioning so that it effectively limits exposures and is employed to diversify risks. In addition, the supervisory bodies will have to ensure that the supervised banks have the best possible access to macro-economic statistics, enabling them to make a reliable country risk assessment. How do the different supervisory authorities cope with these guidelines?

The US system

Within the United States several agencies are concerned with the regulation of banks at the federal level, namely the Federal Reserve Board, the Federal Deposit Insurance Corporation and the Office of the Comptroller of the Currency. The basis for supervision of country risk is the International Lending Supervision Act of 1983, which states in its Section 902 as a general policy:

It is the policy of the Congress to assure that the economic health and stability of the

United States and the other nations of the world shall not be adversely affected or threatened in the future by imprudent lending practices or inadequate supervision.

The International Lending Supervision Act clearly recognises the need to carefully monitor the international exposure of US banks and to evaluate the risks involved. In order that the supervisory agencies can monitor the risk, the banks must submit four times each calendar year information about their international exposure, on a special Country Exposure Report form (FFIEC–009). Furthermore, the Federal Regulators require the banks to file form (FFIEC-009A) which discloses foreign countries in which the bank has loaned in excess of 1 per cent of total assets, or more than 20 per cent of 'Primary Capital'. This form is subject to the 'Freedom of Information Act'. The International Lending Supervision Act recognises the importance of maintaining special reserves out of current income against the risks present in certain international loans or other international assets, when the federal banking agencies determine that such reserves are necessary. The establishment of such reserves is made through the so-called Allocated Transfer Risk Reserve (ATRR). The supervisory agencies determine each year which international loans or assets are subject to the ATRR, what is to be the size of the ATRR, and whether an already established ATRR can be reduced. The Act also states the importance of capital adequacy and asks for international co-operation by the regulatory authorities in order to maintain or even strengthen where necessary the capital basis of banking institutions involved in international lending. The Act even requests from banks specific internal evaluation and approval procedures for international loans exceeding US$20 million.

The US supervisory authorities had already created in 1978 the Inter-agency Country Exposure Review Committee. This committee assesses country risks based on the findings of Federal Reserve Board economists.

Additional disclosures rules exist for banks that have to report to the Securities and Exchange Commission.

So far the US supervisory authorities have been fairly lenient towards US banks with regard to the ATRR in spite of their substantial exposure to Latin America.

The UK system

Within the UK banking system the Bank of England functions as the supervisory authority. In contrast to the United States, the British system of monitoring country risk exposure is done on a case-by-case basis in discussion with each individual bank. Banks must submit to the Bank of England on a half-yearly basis a country exposure report (Form C1). This form requires a breakdown of the total exposure for each country according to borrower, namely banks, public sector and other claims. The banks must further furnish a maturity profile of their exposure, indicate the risk transfers and show their unused external commitments. The Bank of England in addition ensures that the country risk assessment system chosen by each bank is valid and well implemented, through direct discussion with the bank concerned. It also reviews with each bank its reserve position against country risk exposure on an allocated as well as general reserve basis and asks for necessary adjustments if needed.

The Bank of England carefully avoids its judgement regarding the intensity of a specific country risk becoming known outside the special dialogue it maintains with UK-based banks. With such an approach the Bank of England takes into account the differences among the banks domiciled in the United Kingdom regarding their international lending.

The Japanese system

In Japan the Ministry of Finance does not prescribe to banks a particular system of country risk assessment. It leaves it up to the different banks to establish a system that covers their needs. In contrast to most other supervisory authorities, the Japanese system limits total medium- and long-term loans to a single country to 20 per cent of the bank's broadly defined capital. Short-term cross-border lending is excluded from this 20 per cent limit. The Ministry of Finance has, however, been quite flexible with the 20 per cent limitation if it has had to be surpassed because of rescheduling arrangements subject to the International Monetary Fund conditionality.

Banks must report quarterly their medium- and long-term outstandings to each country. In addition, 25 major banks include in their quarterly reporting short-term loans and interbank transactions with a certain number of developing countries.

The Ministry of Finance also prescribes the necessary provisions to be made against certain countries, i.e. so-called risky countries. These provisions vary from 1 to 5 per cent of outstanding loans.

The West German system

In West Germany the supervision of country risk exposure by the Bundesamt für Bankenaufsicht in Berlin is done through a gentlemen's agreement between the supervisory authority and the association of German banks. There are no specific prescriptions about reporting country risk exposure by the banks. It is the banks' management task to evaluate the country risk quality of its exposures. The banks report their exposure once a year to the authority. A consolidated reporting is asked for. The Bundesamt takes a very keen interest in the provisioning against country risk. It compares the percentages applied by the different reporting banks and expresses concern when needed. No co-ordination with the tax authorities has been made so far. No specific prescriptions are made regarding provisions against country risk. The 1984 Banking Law has not changed what is a fairly liberal state of affairs.

The Swiss system

As in most European countries, the Swiss Banking Commission considers it the task of bank management to evaluate country risk and to take the necessary steps to contain it. The Commission, however, has told the banks that the different rescheduling exercises have had an influence on the quality of their assets and that it is expecting corresponding provisions. In January 1983 the Swiss Banking Commission made a survey of 115 banks in order to find out their consolidated country risk exposure as well as to obtain a better view about the way in which banks assess country risks and how they make provision for these risks. The Commission further reports that these exposures are, in relation to the equity basis of the Swiss banks, fairly advantageous compared with the situation in other countries.

In Switzerland the supervisory authority monitors country risk in an individual way. It interferes only when it feels that prudent banking would commend further provisions or an adjustment of the equity base. The Swiss Banking Commission has asked for a 30 per cent provision on the total of all problem country exposures by the end of 1987. In addition, the auditing firms that are allowed to audit banks have been informed by the Swiss Banking Commission about the way banks should report their cross-border exposures. The Swiss supervisory system allows for the substantial differences that exist among the various banks and their operations domiciled in Switzerland.

13

Rescheduling and its consequences

Rescheduling exercises have been events that have signalled for everybody concerned a change in the quality of the country involved. It might, therefore, be worth while seeing what kind of influence and consequences reschedulings have on the balance sheet and profit and loss statement of a bank in order to evaluate their importance. While in theory a rescheduling exercise might be a voluntary one for the lender, it has lately been forced on lenders by borrowers. Lenders simply have no other choice. It obviously must be acknowledged that each rescheduling follows a different pattern. The reschedulings that have involved substantial amounts have, however, shown a similar pattern and turn around the following major points.

Rescheduling repayment of capital

Repayments due during one year or up to a specific date are normally rescheduled over a specific period of time with a certain grace period. Some examples from the past are the rescheduling in 1981 of Turkish debt to commercial banks, whereby the maturity of the rescheduled amounts was fixed at ten years with a five-year period of grace. The Brazilian government rescheduled its medium-term bank credit falling due in 1983 over eight years with a three-year grace period, and Mexico obtained similar terms regarding the extension of final repayment and grace period. This pattern shows that the repayment of capital is usually extended far enough into the future to give the country the possibility to adjust its economy. The reschedulings that have taken place in 1986/1987 have stretched the repayment period even more, namely Mexico with seven years' grace and 20 years' repayment and Argentina with seven years' grace and 19 years' repayment. It should, therefore, be in a position to start repayment of the rescheduled capital at the extended date, or it can upgrade its creditworthiness to such an extent that it can refinance repayment in the international markets. There can be no doubt that the extension of a new grace period for repayment often breeds an optimism in debt service capabilities that is difficult to justify. The inaccuracies inherent in forecasting help to predict such positive developments.

What are the consequences of a rescheduling of repayment of capital for the bank concerned? It normally means that a one-year commitment, which can also be the last year of a long-term commitment, becomes a medium- or even long-term credit. Such a change has first of all an impact on the liquidity of the bank, because it has been forced on the bank. The bank has to rearrange its refinancing of the rescheduled amount. It obviously has the option to incur a maturity transformation risk. With respect to profitability, the rescheduling of the capital due has no measurable impact, in contrast to the fee and spread structure that the extended maturity now carries. Another question is the quality of the rescheduled asset. Does rescheduling mean a deterioration in its quality? This question must be answered in the affirmative, because the alternative to the rescheduling, namely the repayment of capital and the relending of that amount in the international capital market, certainly carries a better risk quality. However, this is true only in view of the possibilities the market offers. The inner quality of the rescheduled asset might even improve, because the rescheduling is normally accompanied by an International Monetary Fund adjustment programme designed to improve the external economic situation of the country in question. Such an improvement is, however, highly hypothetical at the moment of the rescheduling. The lowering of the quality of the asset is generally also confirmed by the provisions often created for assets of this kind.

Adjustment of interest, spread and fees

The rescheduling of debt due carries with it an adjustment of interest, which is usually an upward adjustment for the spread, and a front-end fee for the rescheduling package. Turkey, therefore, tried in vain, for its second rescheduling exercise in 1981, to lower the spread from 1.75 per cent over LIBOR to 1.25 per cent. On the rescheduling of its public debt Mexico had to pay a spread of 2.25 per cent over LIBOR, while a year before the spread was only 0.4 per cent. For Brazil the figures are an increase of spread from an average of about 1 per cent in 1979 to 2–2.5 per cent. In Poland a spread of 1.875 per cent was applied, whereas before the rescheduling Poland commanded a spread of only 1 per cent. However, the most recent reschedulings have seen a reverse of the trend regarding the spreads as Mexico obtained a spread of only 13/16 per cent in its 1986/1987 rescheduling; the same spread was also obtained by Argentina in 1987.

The front-end fee paid in connection with arrangement of the rescheduling even increases these margins slightly. For the bank, therefore, the return on the rescheduled asset is usually higher than the one received before the exercise. The higher return is obviously also an indication of the degrading of the quality of the asset. It is, as a result, probably wise for the banks concerned to put these increased earnings directly into the provisions account in view of the lower quality of the risk, rather than boost their profit and loss statements with them. This should, in addition, certainly be in line with the current outlook of most supervisory and tax authorities.

New money facilities

All the larger recent reschedulings incorporated a new money facility. The new money facility is normally created to finance the liquidity gap of the country in question for the coming 12 or more months after agreement has been reached for the rescheduling. It is normally tied to the facility the International Monetary Fund extends in connection with the negotiation of a rescheduling of debt and is, therefore, often paid out according to the disbursement schedule of the IMF.

These new money facilities obviously have an impact on the liquidity and quality of the assets of a bank, because the bank has no choice other than to subscribe to them. They also influence the profitability of a bank. The application of the funds from new money facilities consists largely in the payment of outstanding interest on the total of the country's foreign debt. It helps, therefore, to keep the non-rescheduled debt current and thus out of the rescheduling. The price for this exercise are new long-term assets of similar quality to the rescheduled capital. This forced lending, as it is also called, helps the profit and loss statement of the bank in the short run, since the banks obtain a return on the assets of the country in question. The non-rescheduled loans remain performing, which means the borrower is paying the asked-for interest on time.

New money facilities are constructed as medium-term loans on a floating-rate basis. They oblige banks to obtain new funds of a medium-term nature, often in a foreign currency. Such balance-sheet-orientated transactions are of a questionable nature, because the banks actually only fund the interest that is due to them anyway and add nothing to the debt service capabilities of the country concerned. New money facilities have a purpose only when the cash flow forecast shows a trend in the future that would again allow for normal payment of interest. Otherwise, they have only negative implications for the banks concerned. They create unwanted assets of a questionable nature, force the banks to commit new medium-term funds, and blow up the profit and loss statement with an artificial profit.

With respect to the maintenance of money market and trade financing facilities, as requested in the reschedulings of Brazil and Chile, the banks did not have to commit new funds. However, part of their assets were blocked and they lost their original freedom to replace these assets by other assets at maturity date. The facilities are also changed in their basic nature since they suddenly became medium-term. The quality of these assets is certainly lower than before the rescheduling, and their refinancing uses the current liquidity of the bank.

Conclusions

The rescheduling of debts has substantial consequences for the balance sheet and the profit and loss account of the banks concerned. It lowers the quality of the assets from the country in question. It can oblige the banks to undertake additional funding operations to maintain the aimed-for liquidity. It can increase the return on assets in a dubious way. The banks should make the necessary provisions for assets from countries in the rescheduling process when presenting their accounts. The rescheduling exercise further impedes the banks' freedom of action.

This is the conservative approach. It can, however, also be argued that reschedulings are in general based on very realistic terms and are thus successful, which implies an improvement in the quality of the borrower. The history of the past 5 years of rescheduling, however, has not given much optimism to that approach.

Part Four
Outlook

14

New lending to countries in difficult financial situations

The need for new funds

With many reschedulings a so-called new money facility was often arranged, which meant that, in addition to the rescheduling of old debts, new funds had to be made available by the lenders. Such new money was applied for different purposes. While part of it was used to pay interest on the outstanding debt, part was also needed to cover balance-of-trade deficits. New funds are always needed when the balance of payments is so negative that it cannot be covered by a drawdown of the country's reserve position. Balance-of-payments deficits are *per se* not a problematic situation; it is their size and recurrence that can create difficulties and, therefore, cause concern among lenders. As balance-of-payments deficits create foreign debt in one way or another, one can conclude that foreign debt in itself is also not a problem; rather, it is its size and the possible speed of its accumulation, as was noted under assessment of country risk. The way in which the debt position and the balance-of-payments deficit move gives an indication of the creditworthiness of a country, which means its ability to obtain new funds from the market.

In this context, E. Löscher[1] has postulated that a certain permanent foreign debt running capability exists for every country, analogous to the fact that companies can also maintain a certain level of debt. This capability is in relation to three parameters, namely competitiveness, financing and cash flow. Competitiveness relates to the current and future international competitiveness of the products and services of a country, especially in view of its foreign exchange earnings potential. The financing

1. Löscher, E., *Souveräne Risiken und Internationale Verschuldung*, Manz Verlag, Vienna, 1983.

parameter is the percentage of a country's participation in internationally available financing instruments, while the cash flow parameter means the amount of foreign exchange that can be reserved for servicing the foreign debt. While the relation of the three parameters certainly influences the possible permanent foreign debt level of a country, as has also been shown in previous chapters, it will not be easy to summarise these parameters in one figure and then obtain the level of possible permanent foreign indebtedness. But it is correct to assume that a country in a difficult situation has already passed its possible permanent foreign indebtedness, because its situation relates to the difficulty of obtaining funds in international markets.

Countries in a difficult situation always need new funds, however, because their balance of payments is in trouble. Such countries can no longer compensate for their negative balance of payments through drawing down their reserves, since these are usually not sufficient for that purpose. They would immediately be completely exhausted. Furthermore, the reserves have reached a level at that stage where they just suffice to overcome the extreme short end of liquidity fluctuations.

As these countries have difficulties in obtaining funds from the international banking community, they have to undertake an adjustment programme to regain creditworthiness in these markets. The correction of the balance of payments, however, requires time and often implies the assistance of the International Monetary Fund. Nearly all the recent reschedulings have followed that pattern. However, only the short-term needs for new funds were met and this was done by exerting pressure and under the sword of Damocles of the 90 days' ruling to declare a loan non-performing in the United States. The 90 days' ruling means that interest has to be received within a maximum period of 90 days after due date in order to qualify a loan as current. Otherwise the bank has to qualify it as a non-performing loan and make the necessary provisions. This rule used as a bargaining means in many rescheduling discussions has lost a lot of importance since the major US and UK banks have made substantial additional provisions on their country risk exposure in 1987. This step was obviously influenced by the declaration of a moratorium by Brazil on its medium- and long-term debt in February 1987. If the adjustment programme brings the current account into balance, in theory no new funds are needed; only the rolling over of the old debt is necessary, which is essentially the aim of rescheduling.

Is such an achievement, that is, a balanced current account, an aimed-for state of affairs and is it a realistic option for the debt-plagued nations? A current account that is balanced means for a nation with a large foreign debt a hefty positive trade and service balance. Such a positive balance is needed to earn the foreign exchange necessary to pay the substantial interest on the large foreign debt. Countries that do not have the blessing of abundant natural resources for export – resources that are fairly stable in price and in constant demand, such as energy – normally achieve a positive trade and service balance over several years only if they can very efficiently produce goods able to compete in international markets. Such a position has been achieved only by Japan and West Germany on a more or less continuous basis over the last ten years. Some far eastern countries, such as Taiwan and South Korea, are moving in a similar direction, and already face a lot of international resistance to their export performance. Is it, therefore, realistic to assume that countries lacking the right natural resources in enough abundance to help them correct their balance of trade can, through an adjustment programme implemented by the IMF, achieve over the long run a positive balance of trade?

Through drastic belt tightening, such programmes can achieve a temporary reversal of the current account of a country. They will certainly correct excesses of a country's economic and financial policies. Their further aim is to return the country to a position that entails enough creditworthiness to make government funds or funds from the international banking community available again. The need for new funds will, however, persist, because only in exceptional cases will the current account show a positive balance over several years, making a reduction of outstanding foreign debt possible. This holds true even more so in the case of countries in difficult situations. Governments and banks should have no illusions about this. There is and will be a substantial need for new funds on the part of all countries that are not in the privileged situation of abundant exportable natural resources, or of having achieved an efficiency in their production and service sectors that helps them to run a positive current account.

Intentionally, no mention has been made of the balance of capital movements in the context of the need for new funds, as this will be dealt with at a later stage.

Another reason for foreign borrowing for many countries has in the past been the financing of budget deficits either in a direct way, or through state-owned entities such as railway networks and electricity companies or the borrowing of local or provincial governments. As long as local markets do not provide enough funds for these purposes and governments are not inclined to change their policies, demands for new funds from abroad will arise from such needs.

It should, however, be every government's intention today to reduce excessively large imbalances in its current account, and foreign borrowing to cover budget deficits, in order to stay within the permanent foreign debt running capability as it is judged by the international financial markets. Only through such a policy will governments be able to avoid what is now called a difficult situation or extricate themselves from such a situation and

137

again be able to cover their needs for new funds. At each stage of a country's development it is in a different position to achieve such a relation in its external accounts. The current development of the demographic situation and social imbalances in most of the countries that are considered to be in a difficult situation make that task extremely difficult if not impossible without further assistance. The global economic and financial environment can partially alleviate this problem by providing an economic growth scenario with a minimum of protectionist measures and an interest structure with real interest at an economically defensible level.

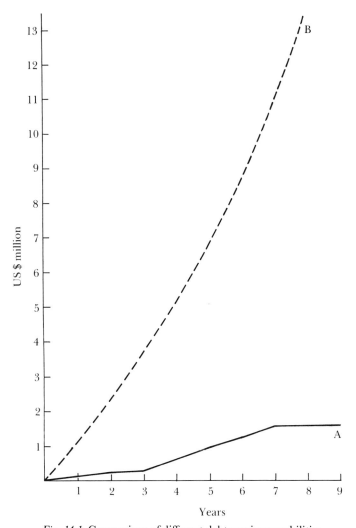

Fig. 14.1. Comparison of different debt service capabilities

Substantial demands for new funds will still be forthcoming from many countries that have or are currently rescheduling their debts or have constantly been borrowers in the international capital markets in the past. The additional need for new funds can usually be kept within manageable limits if debt servicing can be paid out of increased foreign exchange earnings. If, however, the debt servicing of the new funds must be paid out of additional new debt, the situation soon gets out of control, as shown in Fig. 14.1.

The assumption is that country X has a current account deficit of one million US dollars each year over a period of nine years. Curve A shows what happens to the total foreign debt if that current account deficit can be refinanced through a 9 per cent seven-year loan with three years' grace and the debt service can be met through increased foreign exchange earnings. In the case of curve B, the interest on the loans which were taken up to cover the current account deficit cannot be paid out of increased earnings but must also be refinanced by a 9 per cent seven-year loan with three years' grace. Under assumption A, the foreign debt increases from year one to year seven by six million US dollars and then stays at that level. The debt service increases continuously every year but reaches a maximum of about 1.5 million US dollars. Under assumption B, however, the foreign debt increases continuously and already by year eight reaches an amount of 13.3 million US dollars. Every year the refinancing requirements grow substantially, which means the need for new funds.

Countries in difficult situations have to bring their debt servicing capabilities into a proportion that allows them to finance their additional needs for new funds, in principle out of increased foreign exchange earnings. This is possible only when the debt service requirements on the outstanding debt reach a manageable level. To achieve this it is also important to look at total existing debt.

Handling of the existing debt

Since the Second World War, the handling of the existing debt of countries in difficult situations has been fairly uniform, provided they were part of a rescheduling arrangement between the international banking community and the borrowing country or within the Club of Paris, i.e. between governments and the borrowing country. In almost every case, repayment of the debt due was stretched out and new conditions were fixed for the extension. While governments often reduced their interest rates, in most cases suppliers and banks obtained market rates. There have been some noteworthy exceptions: Indonesia, in its rescheduling of government debt US$786 million in 1970, obtained an amortisation period of 30 years with a zero interest rate.

Another interesting example of rescheduling an existing debt was the

London Conference in 1953, which dealt with the foreign pre-war German debt as well as the United States' aid to Germany for the reconstruction of the country after the Second World War. France and the United Kingdom agreed at that time to reduce their claims by 25 per cent and to restructure the outstanding amount in an interest-free 20-year loan, while the United States agreed to reduce its claims by 60 per cent and restructure them in a 35-year loan with a five-year grace period and 2.5 per cent interest. The restructuring of the German debt at such favourable terms was one of the reasons for the strong recovery of West Germany after the Second World War. This is in sharp contrast to the way in which the reparation obligations that Germany had to fulfil after the First World War were handled, even taking into account that reparations are not the same as debts.

The Soviet Union only settled the pre-revolutionary debt with the United Kingdom in 1986 by paying about 10 per cent of the originally outstanding debt, a debt which was not served for 70 years. The People's Republic of China settled its old debt with the United Kingdom after four decades in 1987 with a token payment in order to be able to enter the London bond market. These are not very encouraging developments for the international banking community.

A typical approach to the handling of existing debt in the different rescheduling agreements concluded recently was the inclusion of the debt of only one or two years, i.e. the currently due debt. Depending on the structure of the outstanding debt, such an approach can have a very meaningful result for the borrowing country or give relief only over a short period of time, with the problems arising at a later stage. If a country's outstanding debt is 80 per cent short-term and 20 per cent long-term, the rescheduling will entail a relatively manageable debt service ratio in subsequent years. If, however, the situation is the reverse, the country in question will soon find itself with a higher debt service ratio and have its difficulties compounded. The structure of total existing debt should, therefore, be considered in a rescheduling agreement as is done in the multi-year rescheduling agreements called MYRA in order to obtain not only a new maturity profile but one which the debtor can manage better than the one he had in the past. To look only at the debt due is certainly, among other things, a result of the time pressure under which rescheduling agreements are concluded. Such pressure makes it impossible to assess the long-term aspects of the difficult situation of the countries involved.

The fact that existing debt was not taken into account, with the exception of the debt actually due, was certainly a major shortcoming in most of the early 1980's rescheduling operations. Only through the restructuring of the total debt in view of the capabilities of the country in a difficult financial situation can an acceptable and realistic long-term solution for the

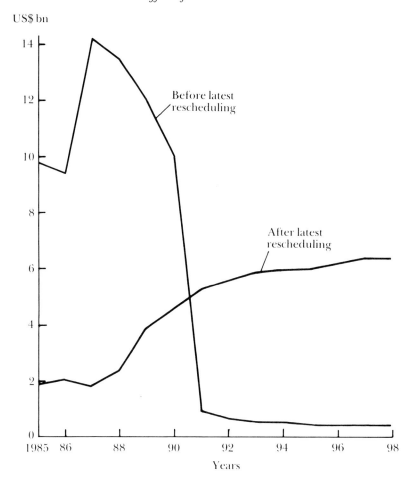

US$ bn

Fig. 14.2. Mexican public sector external debt: amortisation schedule

borrower and the lender be achieved. Such an attempt has been made with the US$48.7 billion package for rescheduling Mexico's debt falling due between 1985 and 1990. It gives Mexico a much more acceptable amortisation schedule, as indicated in Fig. 14.2. This package was again further stretched in the 1986/87 agreement. The debt service ratios for many countries which have not rescheduled their debt through a multi-year rescheduling agreement will, even under fairly optimistic assumptions, again reach dangerous levels within the not too distant future. New lending to countries in difficult situations, however, is certainly easier if the debt service ratio also looks manageable over the medium term.

A more realistic assessment of the long-term capabilities of a country to handle its current debt and the inclusion of the country's need for new funds might alleviate the existing debt in certain cases today.

Lessons to be drawn from the past

As the need of new funds for countries in difficult situations has been proved, it might be worth while to see if lessons from the past can be used to overcome current hesitations to commit new funds. For the time being, new funds are available only in the smallest amounts possible and through forced lending, i.e. the lenders have no other choice.

The lessons for the borrowers

Countries have realised that creditworthiness is the major objective to achieve if they have a constant need for new funds and must obtain these funds in international financial markets, which will continue to be the major source of funds in the future. Creditworthiness is not a situation that can be expressed in figures; rather it is the judgement of lenders based on available information, i.e. on the assessment of the country risk as perceived by the lenders.

This means that countries must adjust their economic policies to the expectations of the international financial community and, therefore, lose part of their independence in this process. In the recent reschedulings, the prescription of the adjustment programmes by the International Monetary Fund to put the country's economic situation on the track of creditworthiness clearly shows such a dependence and, therefore, also the necessity for the countries involved to agree to the programmes. IMF programmes will work only if they are prepared in co-operation with the debtor country and fully endorsed by it. In this context it is interesting to see the different attitudes of governments *vis-à-vis* programmes drafted by the IMF to adjust their economies. While some countries have accepted the interference through such a programme more or less willingly, others have resisted it strongly, Venezuela and Brazil being typical cases of the latter situation. Such interference from the outside, even if it is justified on rational grounds, is politically a very sensitive issue which should be recognised by the lenders. In order to avoid too much interference and overly harsh adjustment programmes that could lead to potential social and political upheavals, countries should give a higher priority to sound management of their economic and financial situation in order to maintain their creditworthiness as consistently as possible.

It must be acknowledged that this task is often very difficult. It is bound to bring with it severe conflicts of interest between internal possibilities and external requirements. To find the critical path along which creditworthiness can be maintained is one of the major and most challenging tasks for the governments of countries that are currently in economic difficulties.

While the International Monetary Fund programmes can help to regain that creditworthiness, it is not the IMF's task to monitor a country's creditworthiness over the longer term. Therefore, countries that still have good creditworthiness but are constantly borrowing abroad should, much more than in the past, orientate their economic policies so that their international creditworthiness is maintained.

The structure and composition of the foreign debt have also played an important role in the recent rescheduling exercises. Dependence on short-term funds from the international network of commercial banks to finance and refinance an ever-increasing foreign debt has proved to be very risky, South Africa being such a case. The floating-rate concept of financing medium-term sovereign credits has been a mixed blessing for the borrowers, as interest rates have become dependent upon the United States' economic and financial policies. The real interest rate for US dollars has moved substantially above the acceptable 3 per cent rate, at an enormous cost to the highly indebted nations. Diversification into different currencies can reduce the cost of foreign borrowing. This should always be considered in rescheduling negotiations.

The reluctance of many countries to accept foreign-controlled investments in their economies has often had drawbacks for their standing. Borrowing countries should learn from this that their debt management and their attitudes towards foreign investments are important issues to consider when economic and financial policies are formulated. The debt/equity swap programmes accepted by several countries are an encouraging sign of acceptance of foreign investments. Within the total programme of foreign financing, governments should make sure that they also incorporate the potential of foreign aid, official funds from bilateral or multilateral agreements with foreign governments, the sources of the World Bank, and the possibilities of foreign export risk guarantee schemes in order to stretch maturities and reduce funding costs. In this context, the International Monetary Fund could certainly play an important consulting role. A further lesson to be drawn is certainly that countries should avoid financing internal current consumption through foreign borrowing. Such borrowing does not create any new source to generate foreign exchange, but increases the debt service burden.

Accuracy and timeliness of information has been lacking in many negotiations of debt that had to be rescheduled. The larger the country and the more diversified its economy, the more difficult it is to gather the correct information in time. The tremendous development of the computer sciences has created the needed hardware and software to perform the information job more adequately in the future. Since creditworthiness is judged on available information, countries with substantial foreign debt should make a major effort to provide the international financial

community with up-to-date data and accurate information on the performance of their economy and on their financial status. Private borrowers have
always been aware that only through accurate and timely information on
their financial status can they qualify as borrowers. The Institute of
International Finance, created by the major internationally orientated
banks, could be the body to help countries devise a system to produce the
information the international financial community needs. It is complemen-
ted by the efforts already undertaken by the World Bank.

The lessons for the lenders

Lenders have learned that the long-maintained umbrella theory, that is, the
umbrella held over the Comecon block by the USSR to protect it from
outside interference or difficulties, does not work in the economic environment as it has in the political situation. Poland and Romania were not
officially supported by the USSR when they had economic difficulties.
However, the USSR interfered immediately when Hungary,
Czechoslovakia, the German Democratic Republic and Poland faced
internal political difficulties. By analogy, one can also ask whether the
European Economic Community would support one of its member states if
it got into financial difficulties. The EEC certainly tries to co-ordinate the
economic policies of its member states so that no country finds itself in real
financial trouble. To assume, however, that an EEC country would always
be bailed out by the other Community members is an assumption that has
not yet been tested. It can, however, be noted that Italy in 1976 received
substantial help from the EEC against the pledge of its gold reserves.
Furthermore, in 1983 the EEC raised important funds to help France.
Lenders should, therefore, have learned that each country has to be judged
on its own merit, which is best done through serious individual country risk
assessment.

Reliance on the judgement of large banks to underwrite international
loans does not lead to a better quality of assets for regional and local banks.
This is another lesson for lenders. They must therefore rely much more on
their own judgement in the future when assessing an international credit
proposal, which means mobilising the resources necessary for an adequate
country risk assessment. Unfortunately, this development has led in the
past years to the withdrawal of several banks from international lending
and not to a better monitoring of cross-border lending. A further lesson is
that sovereign risks have in general not been better country risks than
private credit risks. Experience in international credit analyses can, therefore, be as important as good country risk assessment if a bank would like to
have a well-diversified international asset portfolio, which would also have
to include risks from the private sector.

The different rescheduling exercises have also brought a good deal of disillusionment to the international banking community because they have shown most participating banks their powerlessness and their dependence on the decisions of the large US money centre banks. If the number of banks participating in international lending were maintained or even increased, the lead managers of international credits and issues would have to take that aspect more into account. Otherwise, they will have to take over an even larger part of risk transformation in the future than in the past.

While lenders have by now become fully aware of country risk as a special risk in international cross-border lending, adequate remuneration for assuming that risk has not yet found its way into international lending. Even in a highly liquid market, a differentiation between country risk qualities should always be recognisable. There is too great a tendency to paint a situation black and white, which then leads in international lending to very thin margins, on the one hand, and hefty margins for the countries in difficult financial situations on the other.

Past experience has also shown that when a certain critical point is passed, monitoring of country risk is no longer possible because the bank suddenly finds itself in a locked-in situation. Country risk monitoring should, therefore, always take the future into consideration to foresee possible changes in the risk quality of assets, so that a change of policy and its implementation remain possible.

Country-by-country approach

To speed up the return of countries in difficult situations to creditworthiness in international markets, it is important to review each country separately. Through such an individual approach the parameters for each country are separately analysed and a positive trend can be spotted early. The need for new funds can, therefore, theoretically be satisfied at an early stage of the turnaround situation. Country risk assessment and monitoring along the lines described earlier are the most valuable tools to achieve this.

The country-by-country approach should also be much more in the foreground when a rescheduling becomes necessary. Through the rescheduling agreement and its structure, the country in question should be put into a position that enables it to regain creditworthiness within a sensible time frame at a cost acceptable to both the country and the lenders. This approach still does not prevail today, but can be excused to a certain extent in view of the large numbers of reschedulings that have had to be undertaken recently.

If a country-by-country approach prevails, the question of possible debt relief can be included in the rescheduling discussions without creating prejudice. Countries in difficult situations must insist on being treated individually.

Adequate pricing

In view of the liquid situation of markets in the last few years, pricing of cross-border transactions has been heavily competitive. Margins and fees have been substantially reduced and no longer tend to cover the costs of the risks involved. While no bank can go against the market trend, the profitability of cross-border transactions should be assured. It should no longer be asked what margins must be paid by Sweden or Greece. The margin for the transaction should to a greater extent constitute the remuneration for the risk the lender takes. This remuneration is composed of two elements: the cost of the transaction, including the necessary return on the equity, and the risk premium. The first can be calculated by each bank fairly easily. It will vary depending on funding costs, the cost structure of the bank, and its equity base. Much more difficult is the calculation of the risk premium.

The risk premium must be measured in relation to the potential loss from a transaction, which can be calculated as a percentage of the total amount of the transaction. This potential risk must be recovered over the length of the period of the transaction, which means that a shorter transaction should in theory command a higher risk premium than a longer one if the potential of the loss is judged in the same way. Obviously, markets today have a different view of short- and long-term, and usually consider long-term riskier than short-term. A risk premium for the potential risk can be included either in the margin or in the fee structure. It would mean, for example, a risk premium of 1.05 per cent for a seven-year credit with a 10 per cent potential loss on the principal, or a front-end fee of 5.13 per cent under the same circumstances. As adequate risk premiums are difficult to obtain from borrowers but are necessary to induce banks to new lending, refunding of part or all of the premium on repayment of the credit could be envisaged and provided for in the loan agreement. Adequate pricing, taking into account the specific risk aspects, could certainly help countries in difficult situations to obtain new funds.

It is somewhat discouraging to see that today the intellectual effort of the major internationally operating banks regarding sophisticated pricing structures tends mainly towards devising ever-cheaper instruments for the well-accepted borrower. A rewarding task would be to come up with pricing structures for borrowers in more difficult situations that would be acceptable to the borrower as well as the lender. Unfortunately, the pricing in rescheduling negotiations has become a political issue and, therefore, tends to negate all economic reflexions.

Incentive programmes for new lending

Since awareness of the problems inherent in the heavy debt burden of many countries has become much more pronounced, many proposals have been made to overcome these problems. The proposals deal with management of the existing debt or try to establish a basis that would again enable new lending. In the different proposals for managing the existing debt, a thought that often came up is that an agency should be created to take over the debt exposure of the international banking system and convert it into a long-term debt for the borrower. In exchange for the debt, the lenders would receive bonds or other instruments at face value or at a discount. The late William Mackworth-Young and Felix Rohatyn have been the most prominent exponents of such proposals. The idea is that by making a package of the old debt and by taking it off the international banking community at about book value, the banks would again be willing to write new assets for the countries involved. The borrowers would have their current debt, which they owe to a multitude of creditors, consolidated into one package and stretched over an extended period of time. The price and risk for the arrangement would be borne mainly by the proposed agency, i.e. a supranational institution, based on international solidarity. It seems that currently the political will for such far-reaching solutions cannot be found. Suggestions have been made that one should also look at the possibility of the international securities market, where two constructions could lend themselves to initiate new lending.

One is the Zéro Bond instrument. Through this instrument the debtor country in question can maintain its reserve position until due date and, therefore, build up confidence in the international financial markets. Banks holding these bonds might even be able to sell them in the open market at a later date during the life period. As repayments will be substantial at maturity date, a good maturity profile must be obtained for the country in question. Furthermore, it is uncertain how the different banking supervisory authorities would qualify such bonds since their concern would focus on the question of whether or not they would be considered as performing assets.

Another marketable instrument would be the issuance of bonds yielding a fixed or floating rate of interest and carrying an option for a certain quantity of a specific commodity produced by the respective country at a pre-fixed price. The commodity option could be tied to the interest payment or even to the payment of the principal. The commodity would obviously have to be a marketable one such as coffee, soya beans, copper, etc. Delivery of the commodity would, therefore, be made by the debtor country instead of meeting its obligations financially. The warrants or option incorporating that possibility could be quoted and traded on the leading commodity exchange. Such an instrument would give the lending banks some security and, therefore, incite them to make new funds available.

The authors trying to establish a basis that would enable new lending also see the need to manage the old debt correctly. They consider the role of the International Monetary Fund crucial in establishing a basis for new lending. Its involvement could create an environment of confidence, but how it should be done is interpreted in different ways. Most authors acknowledge the need for the IMF to formulate in co-operation with the countries concerned the economic policies for these countries and then to supervise the adjustment programme of those in difficult situations. Furthermore, it could play an enhanced role by providing new facilities for short-term borrowing or by broadening its surveillance and giving policy guidance to the different countries.

It is interesting to observe that none of the many proposals made publicly to incite new lending have so far had an impact on the international financial community. One of the reasons is certainly that most of the proposals seek help through a third party, which is easier said than done. Furthermore, the different approaches all look for a global solution to the debt problem, which seems not to be the appropriate method since each country is in a different situation.

While global economic growth, relatively low interest rates and the absence of protectionism would help every economy in the world, the solution of the debt problem must be tailor-made for each country. Such a solution can be achieved, however, only through the co-operation of everybody concerned, that is, the borrower and the lender, the commercial and central banks, the different governments and the supranational institutions. The Baker Plan, presented in October 1985 in Seoul by the US Secretary of the Treasury, James Baker, has been a helpful initiative which did correctly focus on that co-operation. Unfortunately, governments were not willing to give it the necessary follow-up. This co-operation must not only ask for understanding among the participants but must also be supported by the will to achieve a long-term positive development, even at an additional cost over the short term. Through such co-operation, the creditworthiness of a country will be established within an optimal time frame. It will also lead to a positive assessment of the country risk involved. No additional incentive programme will then be needed. Currently, available instruments such as cofinancing and lending under a government guarantee have a more prominent role to play in this context, but first let us look at the potential of capital imports.

The potential of capital imports

While new lending will have to provide the largest part of the funds needed by countries in difficult situations, the potential of capital imports to enhance the production base should not be neglected. Capital import in this context means basically foreign investment. As most of the developing countries have growing populations, a fairly low standard of living and an uneven production structure, they represent, theoretically, an interesting market for foreign investments. However, most of these countries have adopted a very restrictive and sometimes even hostile policy towards such investment. It is obvious that these policies have their basis in the growing self-confidence of these countries as well as in the behaviour of some of the multinational companies, which the countries have not found acceptable.

To obtain a good flow of capital imports, countries in need of funds must establish a policy towards foreign investments that also takes the concerns of foreign investors into account. The two major concerns for them are the remittance of the return on the investment and the related administrative bureaucracy. On both accounts it seems that solutions should be possible that not only allow foreign investments but are even attractive to foreign investors. Furthermore, such solutions should obviously guarantee the justified interest of the country concerned. Foreign investment not only helps the balance of payments; it also creates local jobs, wealth, managerial capabilities and production know-how. The debt/equity swaps programmes currently under way in several countries are certainly a useful contribution to the problem of foreign investment. However, they do not provide the country in question with new capital.

It must, however, be understood that foreign investment cannot be attracted simply by a law that is acceptable to foreign investors. It is much more the confidence that the investor has towards a country and its institutions that influences his decisions, because through an investment a long-term commitment is made. It is questionable whether this confidence can be established before a country that is today in a difficult situation restores its creditworthiness with the international financial community. As capital imports are a source of funds for countries in difficult situations, new ways must be explored to activate that source of funds and overcome the current lack of confidence. Bilateral government agreements between a country in need of investments and a country from which investors originate could establish the necessary confidence as well as the safety net investors might be looking for. Furthermore, a supranational guarantee fund for foreign investments could be created by the developed nations which would guarantee the foreign investment under certain circumstances. Such a guarantee fund could be run under the supervision of one of the currently active supranational institutions. It seems that the World

Bank is working on an insurance project for private direct investments.

The potential of capital imports to alleviate the balance of payments must be considered by all heavily indebted nations because of the multiplying beneficial effects for the country concerned. They not only help the balance of payments but can also create new jobs and enhance the wealth of the country. It is understood, obviously, that this issue is politically highly sensitive in most countries. Therefore, it will be up to the countries concerned to take the first step to attract foreign investors. These can also be tailor-made solutions based on bilateral agreements between the governments of the countries involved. A positive attitude towards foreign investment is also a factor that influences country risk assessment in a positive way.

15

The potential of
debt/equity conversion

A new instrument to alleviate the debt burden of the highly indebted nations – the debt equity swap – was created in Chile in 1984. Through this instrument no new financing is undertaken, but debt is neutralised by swapping it into local equity. Thus the need to service debt through interest and amortisation is replaced by the investor's looked-for return. Through a debt/equity conversion, a foreign currency denominated debt is exchanged at a discount into local currency which is then invested in local equity. Such debt-equity conversion programmes have by now been established in Argentina, Chile, Costa Rica, Ecuador, Mexico and the Philippines. Other countries have such a programme under consideration, or work with it on a case-by-case basis. The debt-equity conversion programmes are usually monitored by the Central Bank or the monetary authorities of the country in question.

In order to get a debt/equity swap started, a prospective investor has to be found who is interested in investing a given amount of capital in a local venture in a specific country. This investor will then look to purchase (usually through an intermediary who acts as an agent) an eligible debt owed by that country or a debtor of that country. This debt is normally part of a rescheduling programme. The purchase of the debt is often carried out in the secondary market. The investor and the obligor of the debt to be purchased then enter into an agreement with the institution that is responsible for the debt/equity conversion programme.This institution, e.g. the Central Bank, fixes the rate at which the debt is exchanged against equity. This rate changes from country to country and often depends on the economic importance of the sector where the investment is contemplated.

151

The institution responsible for the debt/equity conversion programme and the intermediary have then to make sure that the respective payments are made and that a correction notice is drawn up under the relevant rescheduling agreement which discharges the original credit.

Debt/equity conversion programmes have to be established in such a way that they conform to the rescheduling agreements and that they ensure equal treatment for all creditors of the country in question. Also, they have to be attractive for the investors, which means that the eligible investors under the programme must be determined in a fairly liberal way and not be restricted to foreign investors only. Furthermore, the conversion rate or fees charged by the government have to make the investment worth while. Debt/equity conversion programmes can thus become a source for repatriation of flight capital. It is obvious that these points are delicate ones as investment policies, as well as attitudes toward foreign investments, are often very sensitive political issues. There is also the concern that debt/equity swaps allow investors to buy cheaply owing to the discounts on the debt, when they might have made the investments anyway.

So far, the Chilean debt/equity conversion programme has been the most successful as it enabled the country to swap about ten per cent of its foreign debt into equity. It is also considered the most liberal one.

Beside the political aspects of the debt/equity conversion programme, the economic aspects of such programmes can also pose some problems. They influence the money supply and can, therefore, have an inflationary impact. However, these factors can be kept under control as the programmes are normally closely monitored by the respective Central Banks. The release of specific amounts each month for such transactions, the use of indexed treasury accounts instead of currency, or the replacement of already funded loans by equity, are just some of the possible measures. In addition, the possible repatriation of the investment, as well as the necessary dividend remittances, can use foreign exchange. Governments, therefore, often restrict the freedom for dividend remittances and repatriation.

So far, debt/equity conversion programmes have not made a substantial impact on the total debt problem. They are still only considered a minor element in reducing the debt burden. Estimates on how much debt has been swapped so far vary, but one can probably say that about US$4 billion of debt have been swapped into equity by the end of 1987. This has to be compared with the over US$400 billion owed to the Western banking community by the most indebted nations. If we want to make an assessment of the potential of debt/equity conversion programmes, we have to take a closer look at the three participants, namely the investor, the seller of debt and the country concerned.

The investor is basically interested if he can see an interesting return for his investment. This is usually assured if the economy is performing well, the market potential for his product line is expanding and the legal and fiscal environment for his investment is acceptable. Through the debt/equity swap, he enhances the return on his investment as he receives the necessary funds at a discount.

The seller of the debt will be inclined to sell his debt at a discount if he feels more comfortable, riskwise, with the money in his pocket than the debt on his book. This is certainly the case as long as Third World debt is sold at a substantial discount and respective provisions have been made by the seller. However, here we already have our first conflict of interest. If the economic and political environment of a specific country improves, the investor will become more eager to invest, while sellers, willing to sell the debt at a high discount, will become scarce.

The countries with high foreign debt, on the other hand, have an interest in reducing their debt burden without having domestic monetary policy disturbed and without giving favours to certain groups of investors. Furthermore, they must follow economic and political policies which provoke the interest of investors, while maintaining the interest of the seller of the debt. Such a policy is probably contradictory in itself. We see, therefore, that it is difficult to realise a debt/equity conversion programme that is attractive to all three parties involved.

It seems that it would be advisable for countries to fix a goal in their conversion programme regarding the amount of debt that the country would like to have swapped into equity. The conversion scheme should then be constructed in such a way that it does not lead to inflationary pressure and should be sufficiently attractive to potential investors. It should aim at least as much at the repatriation of flight capital as to lure foreign investors into the country.

The provisions made by the international banking community on their exposures to countries in difficult situations have substantially increased the potential for debt to be swapped. This opportunity should not be lost and the Chilean case shows that a well designed programme can really help to reduce the debt burden, without touching sensitive political and economic issues too much.

16

Cofinancing

Cofinancing is one of the financing instruments in cross-border lending that in the future could, because of some of its aspects, play a more important role in providing funds to countries in difficult situations. Cofinancing is an instrument that has been developed by the International Bank for Reconstruction and Development (World Bank) but is also used by other supranational institutions such as the European Investment Bank. The reason for cofinancing is that the World Bank is not in a position to fund all the projects that would be interesting for the development of its member countries. It therefore induces member countries to seek funds from other sources for projects of high productivity gain. Such providers of funds are the international banking community, bilateral development organisations and the different export credit organisations. The financing of a project through such a combination of different sources of funds is called cofinancing. The co-operating between the different lenders of funds can follow different patterns, which will be explained later.

Advantages for the lender

Projects that are cofinanced are always selected and reviewed by the World Bank. The projects are, therefore, of a high quality and importance to the country concerned. They are constantly supervised by the staff of the World Bank until their completion. The lenders thus know exactly where the funds are spent and have the assurance that they are well spent. The projects generate a substantial amount of information that helps the lenders to evaluate the risks they face and to better assess the country they are dealing with.

Developing countries attach high priority to their relationship with the World Bank, which is revealed by the fact that the World Bank has never been involved in a rescheduling exercise. It had, however, to put exposures towards several countries on a non-accrual basis and did make provisions against exposures to some countries. Through cofinancing, the risks are lower for the lenders than if they had done the lending by themselves. A country risk that is assumed through a cofinancing project, therefore, has a better quality. This must be taken into account when assessing a specific risk.

Advantages for the borrower

Through cofinancing, borrowing countries can tap a much larger pool of resources. They can realise more of their interesting projects. They can also expand their relations with the bilateral development organisations, the export credit organisations and the international banking community, thereby gaining a better market acceptability. As the World Bank remains a partner, the cost of financing is probably optimised. The increased number of projects that can be realised through cofinancing augments, however, the debt servicing needs of the countries involved, which could be a factor somewhat limiting the potential for cofinancing.

Arrangements of cofinancing

Cofinancing is an interesting tool to finance development projects if it helps all partners. The borrowing countries, the World Bank and the cofinancing entities should all benefit from it. While the World Bank discusses their development projects with the different countries and assists in selecting the most interesting ones, the borrowing countries must decide whether cofinancing should be envisaged or not.

This decision obviously depends on the different sources of funds that are available in view of the project and the standing of the country as a recipient or borrower of funds. While the poorer countries must rely for cofinancing more on the different development agencies, the better-placed countries have access to financing through export credit organisations or the international banking community. It is, however, not the World Bank that selects the modus of the cofinancing, but the country concerned. Cofinancing means a more thorough commitment to a project since it is supervised from the outside. Pet projects of politicians have no cofinancing potential.

The different cofinancing arrangements

The cofinancing arrangements made between the borrower and the different funding units must regulate the exchange of information regarding the project as well as the economic development of the country concerned.

Furthermore, the agreements assign the different responsibilities in view of the project to be realised. The World Bank ensures that the purchasing of the different goods and services needed for the project is done in an efficient way. As the different cofinancing institutions often have different rules regarding the purchase of goods and services they finance, the total volume is divided up into parts that are financed separately. Such cofinancing, which is the most common, is called parallel financing. Each cofinancing entity is clearly visible and retains a direct relationship with the borrower. When the purchasing rules of the different participants are similar to those of the World Bank, a so-called common financing can be chosen, whereby the funds of all the participants are pooled and the purchase of goods and services is done by using an agreed-upon key of distribution.

In order to activate cofinancing, the World Bank has concluded general agreements with national development agencies that establish the general framework of co-operation between the Bank and the respective agencies in view of possible cofinancing. Such agreements have been concluded by the World Bank with several development agencies.

As the international banking community is potentially the largest provider of funds, the Executive Directors of the World Bank agreed early in 1983 on a test programme which should substantially increase the involvement of the international banking community in the financing of interesting development projects. Three different instruments or options of cofinancing have, therefore, been created, all based on the assumption that it is the long maturity associated with the financing of development projects that makes commercial banks hesitate to commit funds.

Through the first instrument the World Bank takes over and funds the long maturities of a commercial loan. These long maturities must obviously go beyond the normal duration of such a loan, i.e. over ten years. The World Bank would then participate with about a 10 per cent share in the total loan. This participation could, however, go up to 25 per cent in order to stretch the maturity profile of the loan enough to better co-ordinate with the cash flow of the project.

Another instrument of cofinancing proposed by the World Bank to the international banking community is based on a guarantee agreement. Against a commission, the Bank would guarantee the long maturities of a loan which has been syndicated among commercial banks, making a longer than normal maturity possible. Instead of a guarantee, the World Bank can also offer a put option for the longer maturities, which would mean that it has to take over that part of the loan for which the put option is established if the commercial bank decides to exercise it. This construction offers the advantage that the commercial banks would keep the loan if, at the put option date, they chose to do so. Besides the option premium, no guarantee commission would have to be paid under this arrangement.

Table 16.1. Cofinancing transactions of the World Bank, 1984–86, in million US$

Year	Sources of cofinancing								Contribution by		Total cost of projects
	Project cofinancing		Public		Export credits		Private		World Bank	IDA	
	Number	Amounts	Number	Amounts	Number	Amounts	Number	Amounts[1]			
1984	97	4,028.1	83	1,978.7	16	942.8	11	1,106.6	4,641.6	1,361.7	21,727.2
1985	107	5,024.2	89	2,635.0	20	1,321.2	12	1,068.0	4,847.3	1,659.7	23,933.1
1986	113	3,525.8	102	2,541.5	11	404.8	4	579.5	3,629.4	1,430.0	23,447.4

Source: World Bank Reports 1985 and 1986.

1. This amount shows the private confinancings according to the financing plans when the cofinancing were decided. It does not show the actually signed cofinancings.

Remark: The number of sources can be higher as several sources are often used for the same project.

Through the third newly created instrument, the World Bank takes over the remainder of a credit based on a repayment in annuities, whereby an amount remains not funded at the end because the interest rate has risen above the level originally agreed upon.

Under this programme, the World Bank can also issue participations in a loan that was originally made on commercial terms.

All these new facilities are valuable instruments to provide new funds to countries in difficult situations. They help the internationally operating banks to contain their country risks. By the end of 1986, the World Bank had arranged under these three new instruments, the so-called B-loans, cofinancings to the amount of US$2.2 billion including contributions from the World Bank to the amount of US$242 million.

Extent of cofinancing

Between 1974 and 1983 the World Bank cofinanced projects in the total amount of US$141 billion. The Bank funded US$33 billion, the cofinancers US$36 billion and the borrowers US$72 billion. While only 60 projects per year were cofinanced during the 1970s, over 100 projects are now cofinanced annually. A change has also been taking place among the different sources of cofinancing. The official government development agencies are still the biggest partners in the World Bank's cofinancing projects. However, export credit agencies and commercial banks are rapidly becoming more important partners of the Bank as shown in Table 16.1.

It can be assumed that in the future cofinancing will become even more important because it is one of the instruments that could help countries in difficult financial situations to obtain new funds. While the project is selected by the country in question, the surveillance of its realisation by the World Bank can enhance its efficiency. The inclusion of the commercial banks will enable the World Bank to pursue a much larger number of projects in view of the additional funding sources. It is hoped that in the not-too-distant future the trial programmes will become part of the standard loan products sold by the World Bank. Furthermore, regional development banks should be integrated in the cofinancing process either on their own or in connection with the commercial banks, as they enjoy a status similar to that of the World Bank and often are even assisted by the Bank. As more and more banks become acquainted with cofinancing, the popularity of this instrument will certainly further increase in view of its positive influence on the quality of country risks.

17

Government-guaranteed lending

Lending under a government guarantee has for many years been one of the very typical ways to support exports of investment goods. The exporter can apply, against a premium, for a guarantee from the appropriate government institution to cover part of the risk coupled with the credit he has to extend to the buyer in a foreign country in order to sell his goods. The ways in which such a guarantee is made available differ from country to country. However, all OECD nations as well as some others have, in one way or another, created institutions that establish such guarantees. These guarantees normally cover country risk and nearly always sovereign risk as well. Sometimes these guarantees can also cover a possible foreign exchange risk. In some countries, the export risk guarantee institution is even concerned with the funding of the credit, whereas in other countries funding is provided by a specialised institution or arranged directly through the commercial banking system.

The origin of these institutions was the need to promote exports; they therefore became at a fairly early stage an important factor for exporters in arranging the financing packages for their exports. The underwriting of country risk and sovereign risk was – and is – especially important for exports to the economically weaker regions of the world, where country risks have always been an issue. The different export risk institutions co-ordinate their work through the Bernese Union. Furthermore, within the OECD a consensus interest rate is established for lending under a government guarantee. This consensus rate, which is the recommended interest rate for such lending, is not differentiated among the various currencies. It therefore helps countries with a weak currency and fairly high interest

159

rates, whereas countries with a strong currency and low interest rates are somewhat at a disadvantage.

While the guarantee scheme is operated like an insurance business, the nationally created lending institutions often have a bank-like setup. The refinancing of these lending institutions, which often belong to a large extent to the banks of the country, is done either by the country's finance ministry or treasury department, or through the international capital markets. Well-known institutions that provide refinancing for government-guaranteed lending are the Oesterreichische Kontrollbank, La Banque Française du Commerce Extérieur and the AB Svenska Exportkredit. Underwriting certain risks, together with the effects of the substantially increased rescheduling operations, has placed financial pressures on many of the export risk guarantee institutions; some have had to set aside considerable provisions or have even incurred losses in the past few years.

The rescheduling of government-guaranteed debt and government debt is done through the Paris Club. The Club came into being in 1956 when a number of European countries met to renegotiate outstanding debts in their bilateral accounts with Argentina. Since then it has become the traditional forum for the rescheduling of government-guaranteed debt and government debt. Table 17.1 shows some of the more recent official multilateral debt renegotiations where member countries of the IMF were involved.

Table 17.1. Official multilateral debt renegotiations since 1984 within the Paris Club involving IMF members.

Debtor country	Date of agreement Mo./Yr	Amount rescheduled (US$ million)
Malagasy Republic	3/84	188
Sudan	5/84	311
Yugoslavia	5/84	802
Ivory Coast	6/84	250
Jamaica	6/84	108
Peru	6/84	845
Togo	6/84	65
Cuba	7/84	204
Zambia	7/84	253
Niger	11/84	25
Liberia	12/84	17
Philippines	12/84	757
Argentina	1/85	2,100
Senegal	1/85	90
Costa Rica	4/85	85
Ecuador	4/85	534
Mauritania	4/85	70
Dominican Republic	5/85	287
Malagasy Republic	5/85	125
Yugoslavia	5/85	625

Table 17.1 – cont.

Debtor country	Date of agreement Mo./Yr	Amount rescheduled (US$ million)
Zaire	5/85	408
Ivory Coast	6/85	210
Togo	6/85	25
Chile	7/85	170
Jamaica	7/85	70
Poland	7/85	11,000
Morocco	9/85	1,200
Panama	9/85	19
Poland	11/85	2,620
Poland	2/86	1,350
Zambia	3/86	370
Mauritania	5/86	60
Yugoslavia	5/86	577
Zaire	5/86	430
Bolivia	6/86	400
Ivory Coast	6/86	500
Congo	8/86	500
Mexico	9/86	1,800
Tanzania	9/86	–
Malagasy Republic	10/86	210
Brazil	1/87	3,274
Gabon	1/87	310
Nigeria	1/87	5,700
Philippines	1/87	870
Morocco	3/87	900
Chile	4/87	140
Yugoslavia	4/87	450
Argentina	5/87	2,100
Egypt	5/87	12,000
Mozambique	6/87	150

Source: Several sources.

From the creditor side the participants are usually the major OECD countries as well as *ad hoc* members that have a credit outstanding to the specific country and would like to take part in the negotiations. It is called a club because there is a very trusted relationship among the different government representatives. The Paris Club does not deal with the official aid programmes of the participating governments nor is it involved in any balance-of-payments support programmes.

The Club meets, theoretically, at the request of the country that seeks to reschedule its external debt. The meeting is attended by all of the official creditors who would like to participate. It is chaired under an informal arrangement by a senior official of the French Treasury. France, therefore, has the role of both mediator and participant. The French Treasury is also responsible for the secretariat of the Club. No formal rules govern the meetings, which are also normally attended by representatives of the International Monetary Fund, the World Bank, the OECD and UNCTAD. In a preliminary meeting the task force of the Club meets without the debtor. The official meeting with the country that seeks debt relief is usually introduced by a detailed report of the country in question, outlining its economic situation, its difficulties and its need for relief. The prospects for its economic development are also reviewed. The representatives of the IMF, the World Bank and UNCTAD then assess from their point of view the balance-of-payments situation of that country, and its long-term prospects. Such meetings usually last for two days and the results are recorded in a set of approved minutes.

These approved minutes then form the recommendations for the participant countries, upon which they renegotiate individually and bilaterally with the debtor country their respective debts and also fix the interest levels for the rescheduling. The Paris Club negotiations take into account the economic and financial situation of the country involved and, therefore, aim for a tailor-made solution.

The rescheduling is, however, done only for the debt due within one year; negotiations with a specific country can take place annually for several years. Conditions obtained from the Paris Club should be a guideline for other debt renegotiations of that country and should not be exceeded. Generally, an IMF adjustment programme must be worked out prior to the Paris Club's rescheduling becoming effective. As the negotiations within the Paris Club follow a flexible but also confidential pattern, there is no publicity. It is left to the debtor country to publish the results of its negotiations with the Club.

Through the Paris Club, OECD governments have created an efficient body to deal with the debt of countries in difficult financial situations. The knowledge thus obtained should enable these governments to follow a more flexible policy in the future than can be expected of commercial banks. They will also be under the pressure of their exporters to keep up their guarantee schemes, especially in the more difficult parts of today's world.

While although next to government aid government-guaranteed lending is usually the most economical source for financing investment goods over a medium- or long-term period, it also has some drawbacks. It often becomes mainly a tool that helps exporters to compete with exporters in other countries and does not take sufficient account of the environment of the importing country. It is, therefore, more product- than project-orientated and leaves the borrower with substantial additional costs until he can really use the product. Furthermore, the nationalistic approach of the exporting country often prevails over the best possible solution. And government-guaranteed lending is, always, only a transfer of risk from an exporter or a commercial bank to the government, without reducing in any way the risk involved in the transaction.

These drawbacks, however, should not reduce at all the importance of government-guaranteed lending in today's environment. The availability of such guarantees is essential for furthering the economic development of the Third World, because it enables the goods that are necessary for building up an efficient economy to be imported. It would, nevertheless, be advisable for the guarantee schemes to be run more like insurance schemes and thus be self-supporting. The substantial deficits which the agencies that provide government-guaranteed lending have suffered since 1984 have led to a rethinking in this direction. The agencies are now trying to provide their services more commercially. One of the ways out was to raise the premiums. This has, however, led to a further decline of their share of export business as exporters are only looking for government cover for the most difficult risks, a development which is not at all strengthening the finances of the agencies because their risk structure is worsening. The different countries are also trying to make their government-guaranteed lending more attractive through better services and better adapted products for exporters. It will be interesting to see how these efforts will change government-guaranteed lending and if they will ever become again self-supporting.

Government-guaranteed lending enables banks to engage in cross-border lending without a country risk being involved. Banks are, however, often excluded from such financing since special institutions take care of it. In these cases, the banks only arrange the transaction.

18

The role of the
International Monetary Fund

Introduction

The International Monetary Fund was created in 1944 by the international conference of Bretton Woods, New Hampshire, USA. At the same conference the International Bank for Reconstruction and Development (World Bank) was also created. The objectives of the IMF at the time were:

- to promote international monetary co-operation by establishing a permanent institution which creates a system of consultation and collaboration for all international monetary problems;
- to help the expansion and harmonious growth of international trade;
- to promote the stability of the different currencies;
- to establish a multilateral system for the settlement of transactions between member states and to eliminate exchange restrictions; and
- to help member states to cope with balance-of-payments problems by putting at their temporary disposal the necessary funds, against guarantees.

In today's international financial environment the IMF's financial assistance to member states with balance-of-payments difficulties has probably become its major task and certainly the most publicised one. While originally this task was meant to be only of a temporary nature, the huge structural payment imbalances that have emerged since the mid-1970s have obliged the IMF to seek new ways to cope with these problems. The question of adequate resources for the IMF has, therefore, been an important item on the agenda of the Executive Directors. The quota system, which is the basis of member contributions to the IMF, also forms the basis for the implementation of many of its policies. The quota system must perform four functions. It determines:

- the member states' subscription to the Fund;
- within approximate limits, the voting rights of the members of the Fund;
- the borrowing rights from the Fund; and
- the share of SDR allocations.

Resources of the IMF

The IMF relies on two major sources of funds: the so-called ordinary resources, which are subscribed to by the Fund members, and the borrowed resources.

Ordinary resources

The ordinary resources are based on the approved quota system. Each member state is attributed a quota according to its economic standing and its ability to support the Fund over the long term. These quotas are expressed in Special Drawing Rights (SDRs) and are adjusted at least every five years in order to take into account changes in the economic situation in different parts of the world. The latest review of these quotas at the time of writing was the eighth, which was agreed upon in November 1983. Through this eighth review, the IMF's ordinary resources were brought to about SDR90 billion. Member countries must pay their quotas within a deadline fixed at each review of the quota. As a rule, 75 per cent of the quota subscription is paid in the country's own currency and 25 per cent in specified reserve assets, currently the SDR. As long as the gold standard was maintained, this 25 per cent had to be deposited in gold.

With its ordinary resources, the IMF faces a certain problem in that most of the paid-in currencies are not freely convertible and cannot be used to help a specific member country with its balance-of-payments problems. Therefore, the IMF asks member states with an adequate reserve position and favourable balance-of-payments situation to exchange their local currencies in so-called 'freely usable' currencies, which are currently the US dollar, Deutschmark, French franc, Japanese yen and pound sterling. The IMF undertakes this exchange each quarter in view of its operational budget in order to be able to cope with the demand for balance-of-payments assistance.

Borrowed resources

Besides its ordinary resources, which are contributed by all member states, the IMF has in the past – and will also in the future – resorted to borrowed funds in order to meet the increased demand for assistance. The borrowed resources including unused credit lines should, however, not exceed 60 per cent of the Fund's own resources. The borrowing policies are currently reviewed when the commitment reaches 50 per cent of the Fund's own resources. The borrowing of the IMF has so far been only from official sources; no borrowing has taken place in international capital markets.

The first such borrowing was undertaken under the General Agreement to Borrow (GAB), which was revised several times. Under this agreement, the Group of Ten (Belgium, Canada, Federal Republic of Germany, France, Italy, Japan, Netherlands, Sweden, United Kingdom and United States) as well as Switzerland currently makes available to the IMF a total of SDR17 billion to assist any of the Group of Ten countries if they should need to 'forestall or cope with an impairment of the international monetary system'. It has, however, now been agreed to interpret the GAB in a more flexible way and make these resources available to all member states, providing the borrowing country agrees to an adjustment programme and that there is a threat to the stability of the international monetary system. In addition, the IMF has concluded a special arrangement with the Saudi Arabian Monetary Agency (SAMA), which will now provide another SDR3 billion under the same conditions as the GAB. Saudi Arabia, however, will not have the full rights of the other participants to draw under the GAB.

During its history, the IMF has resorted to various other borrowings when they were needed to cope with specific situations. Therefore, the IMF arranged in 1974 and 1975 two so-called oil facility borrowings in the amount of SDR6.9 billion. Through these facilities the IMF obtained funds for the countries that were most affected by the oil price increases. In order to increase its general ability to assist countries with balance-of-payments problems, the IMF concluded borrowing arrangements in 1979 to finance the so-called Supplementary Financing Facility (SFF) for an amount of SDR7.8 billion and in 1981 for the Policy of Enlarged Access to Fund Resources (EAR) for SDR9.3 billion.

Through the eighth quota review and the different borrowing arrangements, the Fund has secured for itself an acceptable basis in usable currencies to deal with the substantially increased demand by countries in difficult situations. The Fund's resources, however, are still limited.

The IMF assistance programme

The IMF extends its assistance to member countries under different facilities, which are all based on the member's quota or a multiple thereof. These are the so-called regular facilities and the special facilities.

Regular facilities

Regular facilities are available under the reserve tranche, the credit tranche, the Extended Fund Facility (EFF), the Supplementary Financing

Facility (SFF) as well as under the Policy of Enlarged Access to Fund Resources (EAR). These regular facilities are available under either a stand-by agreement or an extended agreement. While the reserve tranche is freely available and because the first 25 per cent of the credit tranche is largely free of conditions, all the other drawings are available only if an understanding between the IMF and the borrowing country is reached regarding the economic policies and financial adjustment programmes the country intends to realise. The Fund then formalises its commitment to make specific resources available over a certain period of time on the basis of a certain performance.

Under each of these regular facilities the country draws up to a certain amount of its quota. After the seventh adjustment of the quotas, the maximum drawings were redefined and then amounted to 450 per cent of a country's quota for the normal access or 600 per cent including the supplementary financing facility. These drawings are normally available over a three-year period. In individual purchases the different regular facilities are mixed.

Special facilities

In order to extend low-condition assistance beyond the first credit tranches, special facilities were designed to take care of particular balance-of-payments problems. These problems are of a cyclical nature and are, therefore, self-reversing. The most important is the Compensatory Financing Facility (CFF) created in 1963, which extends credit to members, particularly primary commodity exporting LDCs that have problems with their exports due to a sudden price or volume change. This facility is also available for balance-of-payments problems due to fluctuations in the cost of cereal imports. As the CFF is financed by the Fund's ordinary resources, its terms are identical to those of the credit tranche facility.

In 1969, the IMF created the Buffer Stock Financing Facility (BSFF) to assist members in financing their contributions to IMF-approved international buffer stocks of primary products. The BSFF is structured in the same way as the CFF. For both facilities there is an upper quota to draw upon.

The oil facilities created in 1974–75 for members in difficulties because of the oil price hike had their last drawdowns in 1976. It is, therefore, no longer an available facility.

Conditionality

As mentioned earlier, nearly all the facilities to be drawn upon are available only against very specific commitments of the borrowing countries. These commitments always aim to improve the balance of payments over the medium term. This conditionality has no development component. It has its origin in the guidelines for conditionality which were approved by the Executive Board of the IMF in 1979. In paragraph 4 it is stated that

the Fund will pay due regard to the domestic social and political objectives, the economic priorities, and the circumstances of members, including the sources of the balance-of-payments problems.

In paragraph 9 it is further said that

performance criteria will be limited to those that are necessary to evaluate implementation of the program with a view to ensuring the achievement of its objectives.

The performance criteria will, therefore, be limited to macro-economic variables. While these conditions are sometimes criticised as being too harsh or cannot be agreed upon, they are considered by the international financial community as a seal of approval for a change to the better. They are often considered the indispensable basis for the renegotiation of debt by the international financial community. On the other hand, in some of the rescheduling cases such as Argentina, Brazil, Chile and Mexico, the IMF made the availability of its funds dependent on the renegotiation of the private debt, including the provision of new monetary facilities. In the case of large balance-of-payments problems it seems, therefore, that only through co-operation between the two major providers of funds – the international banking community and the IMF – can a solution be found.

Future prospects

Through the active role the IMF has played in the rescheduling exercises, it has assumed the major responsibility for the solution of international indebtedness problems in certain parts of the world. In view of its limited resources, it has had to include the internationally operating commercial banks, which more or less tacitly assume that the adjustment programmes will work. The IMF had to take over this role because of the lack of another supranational institution with similar authority. Has the IMF, therefore, now a global role to play and is it the authority to look to for the solution of the current problems of indebtedness?

The IMF is certainly the institution that was actually formed to assist its member states with balance-of-payments problems. As the economies of the different countries have, however, become more and more inter-dependent, even tailor-made solutions for a specific country can no longer guarantee a successful resolution of the problems. Furthermore, all the adjustment programmes find their limitations in the sovereignty of the country concerned. Apart from the interdependence of economies, the scale of the current problems goes in many cases beyond the reach of even such an important supranational institution as the IMF, whose total resources are smaller than those of the largest internationally operating banks. The IMF has, therefore, to co-operate even further with the internationally operating financial institutions. The IMF needs all the support possible of its member states and the international financial community to live up to its goals. Its efforts should, however, also be supported by other supranational institutions such as the World Bank and GATT in order to complement its efforts.

With respect to country risk assessment, the involvement of the IMF stabilises the quality of country risk. It should even help to improve the quality of the risk through the realisation of the adjustment programmes it prescribed.

19

The Institute of
International Finance, Inc.

When the now well-known international debt crisis began to boil up, the international banking community was suddenly frustrated at being unable to cope with the newly emerging global debt problem. At a meeting of the International Financial Group held at Ditchley Park in the United Kingdom in May 1982 under the auspices of the National Planning Association, First Chicago's Executive Vice-President, William McDonough, proposed the Institute of International Finance, which should mainly help the international banking community to obtain relevant data on a country's performance. This meeting was attended not only by senior international bankers, but also by representatives from the financial supervisory authorities, the International Monetary Fund and the World Bank. The Institute of International Finance, Inc. (IIF) was then officially founded in January 1983 in Washington by a group of 38 internationally operating banks. Appointed as its first Managing Director was André de Lattre, who had worked closely with the President of the World Bank in connection with the International Development Agency's seventh replenishing of funds. M. de Lattre was formerly a high official in the French Treasury and at the Banque de France. It was felt that a European should be the Managing Director of the IIF, which currently has its offices near the IMF.

Article II of the by-laws of the Institute of International Finance, Inc. states that

the purposes for which the Institute is organized are to form an organization of lending institutions to promote a better understanding of international lending transactions generally; to collect, analyze and disseminate information regarding the economic and financial position of particular countries which are substantial borrowers in the international markets so as to provide the Members with a better factual basis on which each Member independently may analyze extensions of credit to public and private borrowers in such countries; and to engage in other appropriate activities to facilitate, and preserve, the integrity of international lending transactions.

Currently, about 180 banks which are responsible for about 75 per cent of all bank debts in non-OECD countries are members of the IIF. In order to fulfil its purpose, the IIF is focusing primarily on three objectives, namely:

– to improve the timeliness and quality of information available on sovereign borrowers;
– to facilitate communications among major participants involved in the international lending process; and
– to foster a greater understanding within the financial community of the future of international lending.

The first objective is realised by creating a country evaluation system which makes available on-line to members the major economic indicators of over 40 major debtor countries indebted to the international banking community. The data available cover the past ten years as well as the current year. This country evaluation system allows user manipulation so that charts, regressions and trend analyses can be made. The system is supplemented by extensive reports on specific countries. The approach is based on quantifying external financial flows between a debtor country and its leading creditors, and plans the analysis of external debt and debt-servicing capability within the context of a country's macroeconomic performance and world economic conditions. A useful link is, therefore, made between the domestic economy and the balance of payment and external debt. These country reports provide, therefore, a thorough review of a country's financial standing. They are orientated in their analyses especially to help the international banking community.

In order to attain the second objective, the IIF is making country visits to obtain additional insights into a country's development. It has further established close relations with the different multilateral organisations and the regulatory institutions of the various governments. A third objective is to establish working groups and task forces to study issues of common concern to the international banking community in order to foster a greater understanding of international lending. Such working parties deal currently with issues such as the 'Future of International Lending' or with 'The Regulatory, Accounting and Tax Treatment of Cross-Border Lending'.

Membership is open to any lending institution that has or contemplates international exposure. The membership fee is in relation to a bank's total international exposure. The IIF is organised according to geographical areas and has in addition a central economic department.

The data and reports available from the IIF are a valuable contribution to the quantitative part of country risk assessment. They do not, however, cover political risks. Their quality and timeliness of the information will add significantly to the data currently available from the different internationally known sources. The IFF needs and has received the co-operation of the country it is analysing. It is still questionable whether it will receive, as time goes by, faster and better data than those the country is currently furnishing to the IMF. It is often not only a matter of willingness to give information but also a question of statistical data compilation capability. It can, however, be expected that the data compiled by the IIF are presented in a way that corresponds much better to the needs of the international banking community, since only one source supplies the needed data. A further problem for the IIF will be the confidentiality of data which a country might release only against certain guarantees.

In order to succeed and to contribute positively to the solution of the many problems and opportunities of international lending, the IIF needs the full support of every country and institution involved in international lending. It will have to produce new evidence and information not currently available from the IMF or the BIS. In its function as a think-tank it would be very rewarding if the IIF could come up with new solutions and answers to the many problems and questions that currently exist between the international banking community and the many developing nations in their lending relationship. Its report, 'Restoring Market Access: New Directions in Bank Lending', is a move in the right direction.

In the context of country risk assessment and evaluation the information furnished by the IIF should, in time, become one of the most reliable and adequate sources of data for the internationally operating banks. IIF information will be an additional tool but cannot relieve the banks from the important question of how much and under what circumstances they will lend to a specific country.

20

Conclusion

Country risk is a commercial risk that became apparent as cross-border lending and investments began to develop at a substantial pace after the Second World War. This development took place not only in a quantitative but also in a geographical way as more and more countries became sovereign states in the decolonisation process. Country risk has its origin in the political and economic behaviour of a sovereign state, which can affect the relationship between borrowers and lenders of different countries, or investors and investments, in a way that is beyond their own control. Country risk has, therefore, a political component and an economic component. In order to contain country risk one must first analyse the different aspects of the political and economic components.

The political part of country risk – political risk – can have its origin within or outside the legal framework of a country. Furthermore, political risk can become apparent through outside influence. In assessing political risk by reviewing the different factors that it comprises, it becomes evident that only a systematic approach that continues over several years can bring meaningful results. Furthermore, the role of the actors has to be considered. The integrated method does satisfy, for the time being, the different requirements of lenders and investors. As the political sciences develop further, more sophisticated methods will certainly be developed and help to better assess the various political risk factors. While in the past political risk was mainly present in the cross-border investor/investment relationship, primarily due to fear of expropriation, this risk has now become more and more important for the cross-border lender/borrower relationship as well. The borrowers' economic performance is increasingly influenced by political factors, since economics and politics have become the inseparable twins of today's economic life. It has, therefore, now become essential to always assess political risk carefully when evaluating country risk.

The economic component of country risk is the so-called transfer risk. The international debt crisis has shown everyone the magnitude of the transfer risks which the international banking system faces today. Bankers have, however, been concerned about transfer risk for a number of years. Several methods were developed to assess transfer risk by evaluating the capability of a country to generate foreign exchange. As information on economic performance is available only for the past, the assessment of transfer risk had to be based mainly on historical figures published with a substantial time lag. In order to improve the assessment of transfer risk, attention has been focusing on the forecasting of the economic performance of a specific country as well as on the timeliness and accuracy of the information available. The interdependence of nearly every country's economy with the world economy, and the variety and complexity of factors influencing its performance, have made significant progress difficult. A combination of quantitative and qualitative factors geared to the specific characteristics of groups of similar countries still seems to be the best way to assess transfer risk in most cases. The choice of the number of different factors will be crucial for obtaining good results, because the larger the number the less evident will be the development of the quality of the country risk. Too many factors tend to balance each other out. In weighting political and transfer risk, the specific situation of the assessing institution should furnish the necessary guidance.

Assessments of country risk are undertaken not only by the institutions that face country risks but also by specialised institutions. These provide country risk assessment in a general way for both transfer and political risks, culminating in rating tables. With the regular appearance of these ratings at fairly short intervals, a fair view of the development of a specific country risk is obtained.

Country risk assessment has, nevertheless, made substantial progress in the past. As its aim is more than ever the forecasting of future developments, it will never lend itself to a fully scientific approach but will remain to a certain extent an art. The development of computer models based and checked out on past experience will, it is hoped, bring new insights into the quality variations of country risks. Unfortunately, however, history rarely repeats itself.

While country risk assessment remains an art in several respects, country risk monitoring is essentially an administrative task. Monitoring country risk should enable an institution not only to limit its country risk exposure but also to follow it up on a continuing basis in order to adjust it whenever the development of country risk assessment makes it necessary. The overall limitation of country risk exposure is best done through the establishment of country limits. It is, however, not sufficient to establish country limits. They must be structured according to maturity and kind of business in order to take into account the potential, as well as the risks, of a cross-border relation with a specific country. These systems to monitor country risk must also identify separately the direct and indirect country risk, so as to allow a complete picture of all the risks incurred to be drawn up. Banks in particular – which usually have constantly changing cross-border exposures – need to establish efficient monitoring systems that clearly indicate their exposure on a continuous basis. Country risk, being a commercial risk, should, according to prudent banking, be included in the provisioning process. Supervisory authorities in the banking sector, as well as fiscal and tax departments, must recognise this and allow or even ask for the necessary provisioning.

For banks, cross-border lending has for many years been an exercise in maturity and sometimes even in currency transformation. As long as the Euromarkets and especially the interbank markets are functioning smoothly, such transformation increases the commercial risk only marginally, but allows banks to take advantage of the opportunities associated with the risk transformation. The question of adequate refinancing is, under such circumstances, not a major issue. Developments in the 1980s, especially the stretching of the maturities in the different rescheduling agreements, have led to a new awareness of the importance of adequate refinancing for cross-border assets. The substantial expansion of the floating-rate note market for bank issues is one of the developments attributed to this awareness. Prudent provisions for country risk and conservative refinancing of cross-border assets have become important issues of international banking.

Banking supervision has also become more concerned about country risk, weighing its implications against the bank's liquidity and solvency. In most cases banking supervision limits its intervention to a review of the country risk assessment and monitoring systems that the different banks are using. Furthermore, data on the actual cross-border exposures are collected regularly for statistical purposes. It would be wise if banking supervision were to continue to limit itself in the future to checking the applied systems, thus not removing from a bank's management its responsibility for the quality of the bank's international assets.

Country risk assessment and the monitoring of country exposure have become important tasks for banks, companies and other institutions in managing their international activities. This book is intended to supply the necessary guidance for the organisation of these tasks. An institution's risk assessment system should make the changing of country risk quality particularly evident. It will be up to each company to establish the system best suited to its purposes. By monitoring country risk exposure, companies can limit and control their cross-border exposure – enabling them to adapt it to their marketing goals.

The rescheduling of cross-border debt has implications for the quality of cross-border assets. Therefore, it also influences the quality of the bank's balance sheet and its profit and loss account. If the rescheduling is successful and restores the country's creditworthiness, it has a very positive effect for the lenders.

The current international debt situation has raised many questions about the future of cross-border lending, specifically to certain parts of the world, as well as about foreign investments in those parts of the world. Since there is not only a need for new funds in order to develop the economies of many of the countries involved, but also a need for them to form part of the markets for the products of the industrialised world, solutions will have to be found to help overcome the difficult financial situations of many of the less-developed countries. The Bretton Woods institutions have to play an important role in this process. The International Monetary Fund bears the responsibility of furnishing guidance and advice on how to improve the balance of payments. It has to monitor countries in difficult financial situations and help them to return to creditworthiness with the financial assistance of the international banking community. This task puts heavy pressure on the IMF because the interests of the borrowing country and those of the lenders often diverge. In particular, the internal political pressure on local governments, based on often unrealistic expectations, pulls the IMF into political discussions that can become counter-productive to its adjustment programmes. The IMF, therefore, needs the unconditional support of all parties if it is to achieve its goals. The World Bank will have to continue to be concerned with projects that help to develop the economies of the chosen countries. The careful selection of the projects will be as crucial as ever in order to enhance the economies of these countries. Furthermore, through its structural adjustment loans, it will help countries to reorganise part of their economies. The different instruments of cofinancing allow the World Bank to multiply its efforts. The Bank's participation assures the cofinanciers of the validity of the projects and of their correct and efficient execution.

In order to satisfy the need for adequate country information, the internationally operating banks have created the Institute of International Finance, Inc. The efforts of the Institute will need the strong support of the countries it is reviewing, since its country data will certainly influence the country risk assessment of banks in the future. This new source of data should focus especially on the timeliness of information.

Country risk assessment and monitoring will play an important role in future in the allocation of the various resources available to build and expand the economies of the LDCs. Therefore, both the lender or investor and the borrower will have to take this into account. The latter will have to direct and adjust his economic policies if he needs funds from the international financial community. Politicians in all countries that depend substantially upon the inflow of foreign funds must be concerned about the quality of the international creditworthiness of their countries. Such an awareness could generate a significant improvement in the country risk of many countries and stop the deterioration of the risk in others. Furthermore, they will also have to include in their reflections the position of the investor as he can contribute, too, to a country's development. Debt/equity conversion programmes are, in this connection, an interesting tool.

As such developments do not yet seem to be forthcoming, it will be necessary for the prudent international banker and investor to continue to watch the international economic and political environment closely through their country risk assessment systems, monitoring their exposure carefully in order to optimise the risk composition of their cross-border lending or investments.

Bibliography

Books

Brau, E., Williams, R. C., Keller, P. M. and Nowak, M., *Recent Multilateral Debt Restructurings with Official and Bank Creditors*, Occasional Paper No. 25, International Monetary Fund, Washington, DC, December 1983.

Calverley, J., *Country Risk Analysis*, Butterworths, London, 1985.

Ensor, Richard, *Assessing Country Risk*, London, Euromoney Publications, 1981.

Friedman, Irving S., *The World Debt Dilemma: Managing Country Risk*, Council for International Banking Studies, Washington, DC and Robert Morris Associates, Philadelphia, PA, 1983.

Group of Thirty, *Risks in International Lending*, Group of Thirty, New York, 1982.

Hardy, Chandra S., *Rescheduling Developing Country Debt, 1956–1981, Lessons and Recommendations*, Overseas Development Council, Washington, DC, 1982.

Löscher, E., *Souveräne Risiken und Internationale Verschuldung*, Manz Verlag, Vienna, 1983.

Mendelsohn, M. S., *Commercial Banks and the Restructuring of Cross-border Debt*, Group of Thirty, New York, 1983.

The Mexican Debt and Payment Crisis, International Center for Monetary and Banking Studies, Geneva, 1983.

Nagy, Pancras J., *Country Risk, How to Assess, Quantify and Monitor it*, Euromoney Publications, revised edition, London, 1984.

Overholt, William H., *Political Risk*, Euromoney Publications, London, 1983.

Sofia, A. Zuheir, *External Debt of Developing Countries, its Application to Country Risk Analysis*, Library thesis, Columbus, Ohio, 1978.

Soros, G., *The International Debt Problem, Diagnosis and Prognosis*, Morgan Stanley, New York, 1983.

Periodicals: Part One

Anderson, T., 'The Year of the Rescheduling', *Euromoney*, August 1982.

Bibliography

Anderson, T., 'More Models than Vogue Magazine', *Euromoney*, November 1982.

Burton, F. N. and Inoue, H., 'Country Risk Evaluation Methods: A Survey of System in Use', *The Banker*, January 1983.

Calverley, J., 'How the Cash Flow Crisis Floored the LDCs', *Euromoney*, August 1982.

Clausen, A. W., 'Let's Not Panic About Third World Debts', *Harvard Business Review*, November/December 1983.

Dale, R. S., 'Country Risk and Bank Regulation', *The Banker*, March 1983.

de Vries, B. A., 'International Ramifications of the External Debt Situation', *The Amex Bank Review*, no. 8, November 1983.

Dini, L., 'Where the International Financial System Needs Strengthening', *The Banker*, September 1983.

Dizard, J. W., 'The End of Let's Pretend', *Fortune*, 29 November 1982.

Fratianni, M., 'International Debt Crisis: Policy Issues', *The Banker*, August 1983.

Lomax, D., 'The Recycling Folly', *The Banker*, August 1982.

McMahon, K., 'International Debt Problems – A Progress Report', Bank of England *Quarterly Bulletin*, June 1983.

Quek Peck Lim, 'The Borrower's Trump Card is his Weakness', *Euromoney*, October 1982.

Reading, B., 'There are Debtors on our Doorstep', *Investors Chronicle*, 1 July 1983.

Schröder, K., 'Rescheduling the Debts of CMEA Countries', *Aussenpolitik*, vol. 34, no. 2, 1983.

Shaw, E. R., Howcroft, J. B. and Gill, C. C., 'Identifying International Lending Risk', *The World of Banking*, March/April 1982.

Taylor, M. G., 'Time for a New Departure', *Euromoney*, November 1982.

Speech: Part One

Angermueller, H. H., 'LDC Debt, the "Bailout" that Isn't', Citibank, Annual Dinner, 7 February 1983.

Periodicals: Part Two

Baird, J., 'Where Did Country Risk Analysts Go Wrong?', *Institutional Investor*, May 1983.

Bird, G., 'New Approaches to Country Risk', *Lloyds Bank Review*, October 1986.

Dale, R., 'The Geobanking Gravy Train', *International Currency Review*, vol. 14, no. 5, December 1982.

Dewett, P. and Madura, J., 'How Banks Assess Country Risk', *World of Banking*, January/February 1986.

Feder, G. and Just, R. E., 'A Study of Debt Servicing Capacity Applying Logit Analysis', *Journal of Development Economics*, 3/1977.

Gonzalez, E., 'Call a Country a Company and it Looks Better', *Euromoney*, February 1983.

Heenan, D. A. and Addleman, R., 'Quantitative Techniques for Today's Decision Makers', *Harvard Business Review*, May/June 1976.

Kinkead, G., 'Banks Tell (Not Quite) All About Foreign Loans', *Fortune*, 29 November 1982.

179

Bibliography

Kraar, L., 'The Multinationals Get Smarter About Political Risks', *Fortune*, 24 March 1980.

Krayenbuehl, T. E., 'How Country Risk Should Be Monitored', *The Banker*, May 1983.

Lascelles, D., 'U.S. Bank Regulation after the Debt "Crisis"', *The Banker*, January 1983.

Lomax, D., 'Sovereign Risk Analysis Now', *The Banker*, January 1983.

Nagy, P., 'A Quality Indicator for the International Loan Portfolio', *Euromoney*, April 1980.

Nisse, Jason, 'The Benefits of Hindsight', *The Banker*, July 1987.

Papadopoulos, P., 'Measuring and Evaluating Country Risk', *Canadian Banker*, vol. 90, no. 6, December 1983.

Papadopoulos, P., 'Alternative Systems of Country Risk Evaluation', *Canadian Banker*, vol. 91, no. 1, February 1984.

Robinson, J. N., 'Is it Possible to Assess Country Risk?', *The Banker*, January 1981.

Rummel, R. J. and Heenan, D. A., 'How Multinationals Analyse Political Risk', *Harvard Business Review*, January/February 1978.

Senkiw, Roman I., 'Using Country Risk Assessments in Decision-Making', *The Journal of Commercial Bank Lending*, August 1980.

Sofia, A. Z., 'How to Rationalize Country Risk Ratios', *Euromoney*, September 1979.

Thompson, J. K., 'The Poor Man's Guide to Country Risk', *Euromoney*, July 1981.

Yassukovich, S. M., 'Eurobonds and Debt Rescheduling', *Euromoney*, January 1982.

Periodicals: Part Three

Albert, A., 'Fed Adopts Foreign Loan Reserves', *American Banker*, 3 February, 1984.

Cooke, P., 'The Basle "Concordat" on the Supervision of Banks' Foreign Establishments, *Aussenwirtschaft*, 39th year (1984), nos. 1/2.

'Country Risk and Bank Head Office Responsibility for Foreign Branch Deposits', *International Currency Review*, vol. 13 (1982), no. 6.

Montagnon, P., 'Banks Top Fresh Medium-Term Funds', *Financial Times*, 18 March 1983.

Quinn, B., 'Supervisory Aspects of Country Risk', *Bank of England Quarterly Bulletin*, June 1984.

Stevenson III, J. J., 'Funding Problems in Sovereign Debt Rescheduling', *International Financial Law Review*, November 1982.

'Those Citibank Deposits', *International Currency Review*, vol. 15 (1984), no. 1.

Wood, P. R., 'Debt Priorities in Sovereign Insolvency', *International Financial Law Review*, November 1982.

Periodicals: Part Four

Bindert-Bogdanowicz, Ch. 'Debt Rescheduling: The Struggle to Cope', *Revue de la Banque*, June/July 1983.

'Cofinancing', The World Bank, Washington, DC, September 1983.

Dale, R., 'A Better Way out of the World Debt Crisis', *Financial Times*, 31 August 1983.

'Debt Rescheduling: What does it mean?', *Finance and Development*, September 1983.

Bibliography

Emerson, T., 'Argentina's Debt: The View from Buenos Aires', *The Banker*, April 1984.

Fierman, J., 'Fast Bucks in Latin Loan Swaps', *Fortune*, 4 August 1987.

French, M., 'Swapping Debt – Just Hot Air?', *Euromoney*, May 1987.

Glynn, L., 'Is Time Running out for Brazil?', *Institutional Investor*, April 1984.

Gorman, Derek, 'The IMF: Its Financial Role', *Barclays Review*, February 1984.

Guth, W., 'International Debt Crisis: The Next Phase', *The Banker*, July 1983.

Mendelsohn, M. S., 'International Debt Crises: The Practical Lessons of Restructuring', *The Banker*, July 1983.

Mendelsohn, M. S., 'The Wrong Way to Tackle Debt', *The Banker*, March 1987.

Nowzad, B., 'The Extent of IMF Involvement in Economic Policy-Making', *The Amex Bank Review Special Papers*, no. 7, September 1983.

Ollard, W., 'The Debt Swappers', *Euromoney*, August 1986.

Rhodes, W. R., 'A Success Formula for Latin America', *Institutional Investor*, March 1984.

Rommel, Thierry, 'The Debt-Strategy Revisited: Are New Initiatives Required?', *Revue de la Banque*, May 1987.

Sandler, L., 'Can Crisis Cofinancing Save the World?', *Institutional Investor*, February 1983.

Sandler, L., 'The Great Debate over LDC Loan Swapping', *Institutional Investor*, May 1984.

Schubert, M., 'Trading Debt for Equity', *The Banker*, February 1987.

'The Financial Structure and Operations of the International Monetary Fund', Bank of England *Quarterly Bulletin*, December 1983.

Wels, Alena, 'The "Ditchley Institute" Maps Out its Route', *The Banker*, November 1983.

Welt, Lev., 'Untying those Blocked Funds', *Euromoney*, May 1987.

Index